Connecting History

Higher

The Wars of Independence
1249–1328

Michèle S. Duck

The Publishers would like to thank the following for permission to reproduce copyright material.

Photo credits

Photos reproduced by the permission of: **p.vi** © Ulmus Media/Shutterstock; **p.1** © Ulmus Media/Shutterstock; **p.3** © Heritage Image Partnership Ltd /Alamy Stock Photo; **p.4** National Records of Scotland; **p.22** © Ulmus Media/Shutterstock; **p.22** The Picture Art Collection/Alamy Stock Photo; **p.30** Mike Brooks © Queen's Printer for Scotland, National Records of Scotland, SP13/7; **p.31** © Cameron Cormack/Alamy Stock Photo; **p.34** © Ulmus Media/Shutterstock; **p.38** © Classic Image/Alamy Stock Photo; **p.41** © William McKelvie/Stock Adobe; **p.44** © British Library Board. All Rights Reserved/Bridgeman Images; **p.45** © Archiv der Hansestadt Lübeck, 7.1-3.1 Anglicana 12a; **p.51** © chrisdorney/Stock Adobe; **p.53** © Ulmus Media/Shutterstock; **p.56** © GL Archive/Alamy Stock Photo; **p.65** © British Library Board. All Rights Reserved/Bridgeman Images; **p.71** © The Print Collector/Alamy Stock Photo; **p.75** National Records of Scotland.

Acknowledgements

p.8 extract from 'A kingdom in crisis: Scotland and the Maid of Norway', *The Scottish Historical Review*, Vol. 69, No. 188, Part 2: Studies Commemorative of the Anniversary of the Death of the Maid of Norway (October 1990), 136. Published by Edinburgh University Press; **p.30** extract from *Robert the Bruce, King of Scots* by Michael Penman, published by Yale University Press. Copyright © 2014 Michael Penman. Reprinted by permission of Yale Representation Ltd.; **pp.31 & 44** two extracts from *Scotland: A New History* by Michael Lynch. Copyright © Michael Lynch, 1991, 1992; published by Century Ltd 1991, Pimlico 1992. Reprinted by permission of The Random House Group Limited; **p.43** extract from *William Wallace: The Man and the Myth* by Chris Brown, published by The History Press. Copyright © Chris Brown, 2005, 2007, 2014. Reproduced by permission of The History Press.

Every effort has been made to trace all copyright holders, but if any have been inadvertently overlooked, the Publishers will be pleased to make the necessary arrangements at the first opportunity.

Although every effort has been made to ensure that website addresses are correct at time of going to press, Hodder Gibson cannot be held responsible for the content of any website mentioned in this book. It is sometimes possible to find a relocated web page by typing in the address of the home page for a website in the URL window of your browser.

Hachette UK's policy is to use papers that are natural, renewable and recyclable products and made from wood grown in well-managed forests and other controlled sources. The logging and manufacturing processes are expected to conform to the environmental regulations of the country of origin.

Orders: please contact Hachette UK Distribution, Hely Hutchinson Centre, Milton Road, Didcot, Oxfordshire, OX11 7HH. Telephone: +44 (0)1235 827827. Email education@hachette.co.uk Lines are open from 9 a.m. to 5 p.m., Monday to Friday. You can also order through our website: www.hoddereducation.co.uk. If you have queries or questions that aren't about an order, you can contact us at hoddergibson@hodder.co.uk

© Michèle S. Duck 2022
First published in 2022 by
Hodder Gibson, an imprint of Hodder Education
An Hachette UK Company
50 Frederick Street
Edinburgh, EH2 1EX

Impression number	5	4	3	2	1
Year	2026	2025	2024	2023	2022

All rights reserved. Apart from any use permitted under UK copyright law, no part of this publication may be reproduced or transmitted in any form or by any means, electronic or mechanical, including photocopying and recording, or held within any information storage and retrieval system, without permission in writing from the publisher or under licence from the Copyright Licensing Agency Limited. Further details of such licences (for reprographic reproduction) may be obtained from the Copyright Licensing Agency Limited, www.cla.co.uk

Cover photo © Ulmus Media/Shutterstock
Illustrations by Integra Software Services Pvt. Ltd., Pondicherry, India
Typeset in 11/13pt ITC Berkeley Oldstyle Std Book by Integra Software Services Pvt. Ltd., Pondicherry, India
Produced by DZS Grafik, Printed in Bosnia & Herzegovina

A catalogue record for this title is available from the British Library.

ISBN: 978 1 3983 4538 6

Contents

Introduction		vi
Chapter 1	Alexander III and the succession problem in Scotland, 1286–92	1
Chapter 2	John Balliol and Edward I, 1292–96	22
Chapter 3	William Wallace and the Scottish resistance	34
Chapter 4	The rise and triumph of Robert Bruce VII	53
Index		79

Welcome to Connecting History!

The aim of this series is to provide rich and accessible information that will help learners, teachers and lecturers to get the most out of History. The series has dedicated resources for National 4/National 5 and Higher History. It sparks interest, provides the right level of detailed information and is straightforward to access through its consistent and clear structure.

Overall, Connecting History is designed to provide a fresh approach to the study of History. The series is:

- **Consistent.** The content of each book is structured in a similar way around the key themes of the course. This clear structure will make it easy to find what you need when studying History. Indeed, all books in the series are designed this way, so that every book, for every unit, is equally accessible. This will make it quick and easy to find the information that learners and teachers need, whether revising, extending study or planning a lesson.
- **Focused.** Up-to-date course specifications have been used to create these books. This means that it is easy for learners and teachers to find information and provides assurance that the books offer complete coverage of the examinations, as well as general study. This means that you will not have to read through multiple long texts to collate information for one content area – our authors have done this already.
- **Relevant.** The importance and significance of each area to your understanding of our world and history has been clearly set out. Background sections in each chapter capture issues in their entirety, and sub-sections go into detail on key issues, with a number of sources and interpretations included. These texts go beyond the standard material that has been in circulation for a while and bring in new opinions, evidence and historical scholarship to enrich the study of History. We hope that this will continue to foster an ability not only to be highly successful in History, but also to inspire a love of the subject.
- **For today.** These units are not just about the past, they are about today. Themes of social justice, equality, change and power are all discussed. The most up-to-date research has been reflected by our authors, old interpretations have been challenged and we have taken a fresh look at the importance of each unit. We firmly believe that it is impossible to understand the present without a firm understanding of the past.
- **For tomorrow.** This series prepares learners for the future. It provides the knowledge, understanding and skills needed to be highly successful in History exams. Perhaps just as importantly, these books help learners to be critical and curious in their engagement with History. They challenge readers to go beyond the most obvious or traditional narratives and get to the bottom of the meaning and importance of the past. These skills will make readers not only successful learners, but also effective and responsible citizens going forward.

We hope that you enjoy using the Connecting History series and that it fosters a love of History, as well as exam success.

Several units in this series are supported by digital resources for planning, revision, extension and assessment in Boost, our online learning platform. These will be updated annually to reflect recent course and assessment updates. If the nature of the assessment changes, or the skills are tweaked, fear not, our digital resources will be updated to reflect this. To find out more about this series – including the Boost resources and eBooks – visit **www.hoddergibson.co.uk/connecting-history**

Our academic reviewers

Every Connecting History textbook has been reviewed by a member of our Academic Review Panel. This panel, co-ordinated by our Academic Advisory Board, consists of nine Academic Editors with links to the University of Glasgow across a range of historical specialisms.

The Academic Editors have reviewed our text, looking at:

- historiography, including the latest research and scholarship
- content, especially that it is culturally appropriate, up to date and inclusive
- material, for accuracy and to see that it states facts clearly.

Academic Review Panel	Units reviewed
Professor Dauvit Broun, Professor of Scottish History	Higher: The Wars of Independence, 1249–1328 National 4 & 5: The Wars of Independence, 1286–1328
Dr Rosemary Elliot, Senior Lecturer (Economic & Social History)	Higher: The Impact of the Great War, 1914–1928 National 4 & 5: The Era of the Great War, 1900–1928
Dr Shantel George, Lecturer (History)	National 4 & 5: The Atlantic Slave Trade, 1770–1807
Dr Ewan Gibbs, Lecturer in Global Inequalities (Economic & Social History)	Higher: Britain, 1851–1951
Dr Lizanne Henderson, Senior Lecturer in History (Interdisciplinary Studies)	Higher: Migration and Empire, 1830–1939 National 4 & 5: Migration and Empire, 1830–1939
Dr Mark McLay, Lecturer in American History	Higher: USA, 1918–1968 National 4 & 5: The Atlantic Slave Trade, 1770–1807
Dr Alexander Marshall, Senior Lecturer (History)	Higher: Russia, 1881–1921 National 4 & 5: Red Flag: Lenin and the Russian Revolution, 1894–1921
Professor Ray Stokes, Chair of Business History (Economic & Social History)	Higher: Germany, 1815–1939
Dr Danielle Willard-Kyle, Research Associate	National 4 & 5: Hitler and Nazi Germany, 1919–1939

Academic Advisory Board	Dr Karin Bowie, Senior Lecturer in Scottish History, University of Glasgow
	Dr Philip Tonner, Lecturer in Education (History), University of Glasgow

Introduction

The Scottish Wars of Independence were a series of battles fought by Edward I of England, his successors and members of the Scottish nobility between 1286 and 1328. The people and events have been shrouded in myth and legend for generations and their exploits, romanticised and embellished, have come to shape Scotland's identity as a nation. Tales of the battles and the men who fought in them have been retold and popularised by films like *Braveheart* and *Outlaw King*. These films portray blue-faced Highland armies, clad in billowing tartan kilts, playing the bagpipes as they run through heather headlong into the armoured knights of the English forces. However, this book will help you begin to explore what we really know about the Scottish Wars of Independence. Information about this period comes from sources written for entertainment, some of which only exist in part, or sometimes written many years after events. So, historians are sometimes still not in complete agreement about what they tell us – this is reflected in this book. The memory of the Wars still informs the discussion about political unity today, and so it is important to understand the reality, as much as possible, of the events that took place.

Scotland in the thirteenth century was vastly different from the place we know today. The King of Scots governed with the help of powerful families from across the country. There was not one **parliament** building or regular parliaments. Travel was expensive and so government was conducted all over the country. Most people would never leave their local area. Although there were some well-known routes through the kingdom, there were no smooth roads and those who travelled did so by foot, cart, horseback or boat. Travel by boat was by far the fastest way to get around; across seas, between lochs and along rivers. Merchants took their supplies by boat between markets, and armies were supplied by ships from the sea. Scotland actively traded with France and England and exported wool in return for imports of wine and other luxuries.

There had been strong social links between the kingdoms of Scotland and England. Before the Wars, subjects of the King of Scots had been able to hold lands in England, and English subjects were able to hold lands in Scotland. For much of the period, the Wars of Independence were as much a civil war as they were a war against the overlordship of Edward I. Scottish nobles fought for and against both sides, and between themselves, in an effort to maintain their own power and prestige. However, after 1314, cross-border land ownership was forbidden by the Scottish King and the nobility had to choose to keep either their land in Scotland or their land in England. By 1328, Scotland had established itself as an independent kingdom without English influence under one King. But how and why did this happen?

To help us, we must answer the following questions: why was Scotland thrown into a succession crisis after the death of Alexander III? What role did Edward I play in choosing the next King of Scots? Why did King John Balliol have difficulties ruling Scotland? How did Scotland resist English overlordship and how did Edward assert it? What was William Wallace's contribution to the resistance and how effective was other resistance? Why was Robert Bruce VII, popularly known as Robert the Bruce, able to rise to become the King of an independent Scotland?

The answers to these questions are included in the following pages. Note, there is not one simple, straightforward answer to each. Instead, we will be dealing with evidence-based arguments. You will use the straightforward and clear structure to target different sections of this text. This will allow you to find the relevant, accurate and developed knowledge needed to support a convincing argument that answers a key issue. You will also find explanations and analysis of these arguments, helping to integrate this information in source question responses. Finally, activities at the end of each chapter will help develop source skills and nurture the understanding needed to write clear and well-reasoned responses.

Whether revising for an examination, writing an assignment or deepening your understanding of a particular area, this book will help you. Each chapter covers a specific issue that could appear as a source-handling question and the information contained over the following pages will support you in writing a powerful response.

Good luck!

Chapter 1

Alexander III and the succession problem in Scotland, 1286–92

The aim of this chapter is to introduce the nature of the succession problem in Scotland between 1286 and 1292. It will focus on the political disputes of those who thought they should be the next King of Scots. It will also set out the problems that this caused in Scotland.

LINK TO EXAM

Higher

Key issue 1: An evaluation of the reasons why there was a succession problem in Scotland, 1286–92

Background

King Alexander III's reign as King of Scots was known as a 'Golden Age'. It was a time of relative peace and economic growth in Scotland. However, Alexander died in 1286 with no surviving children. His death, and the political problems that followed, have become known in Scottish history as 'the succession crisis'.

This is not to say that Scotland was now ungovernable. Alexander's wife, Yolande, was pregnant when he died. To maintain stability until Yolande gave birth, Scotland was run by a group of Guardians. There is every indication that the government of the Guardians was successful. They brought in new legislation, negotiated treaties and quelled internal disputes. However, Yolande and Alexander's baby was **stillborn**. Following this, the next named heir to the throne, Margaret the Maid of Norway, died on her way to Scotland from Norway. Following Margaret's death, Scotland was launched into political crisis.

Competition between nobles with rival claims to the throne placed Scotland on the brink of civil war. To avoid conflict, Edward I of England was asked for aid. His actions and decisions at Norham and Berwick contributed to the succession crisis in the kingdom of Scotland and the rise of John Balliol II as the new King of Scots.

It is important to note that the government and society of Scotland in the late thirteenth century was structured around the political authority of the King. Kings had significant political and legal powers and were the ultimate authority in their kingdoms. However, they also needed to maintain the loyalty of **lords**, **barons**, nobles and the population more generally. Kings devolved powers to their nobles, and in return expected loyalty and support. This was a complex political relationship, and powerful families often competed for the most prestigious roles within a kingdom. Status and position were often marked with land ownership, and **tenant farmers** paid rents and provided military service to the lords and barons who controlled the regions in which they lived. Scotland, like the rest of Europe, was a deeply religious place, and the Roman Catholic Church, with the Pope at its head, exercised significant power.

At the centre of this social and political structure was a King whose line would normally be extended through his eldest son. With this line threatened and eventually broken, Scotland was plunged into a so-called 'succession crisis'. Given that such power was centred in the King's hands, the question that emerged was: who should be the next King of Scotland? The resolution of this question, and the conflicts it raised, are the subject of this chapter's discussion.

It is helpful to think of this period in three distinct phases. The first was from April to November 1286. Alexander's wife, Yolande, was pregnant and so everything was on hold. If a boy had been born, there would have been no crisis of succession: there would have been a political challenge about how to govern, but the Guardians were already in place to deal with this challenge. The second phase was from November 1286 to October 1290. Yolande's stillbirth meant that Margaret the Maid of Norway was generally acknowledged as the heir. The only people who disagreed with this were the Bruces in the south-west of Scotland. Their short-lived rebellion did not really amount to a national crisis, but it was certainly a regional one. On the whole, while there were political problems, this period is not normally understood as a succession crisis. Finally, when Margaret's death became known in October 1290, there was definitely a crisis of succession. Civil war beckoned and help had to be sought from Edward I of England.

Why did Scotland face a succession problem between 1286 and 1292?

For the exam, it is important to understand the reasons why Scotland faced problems over the succession to the throne. In order to do this, it is necessary to understand the impact of the death of Alexander III and the competing aims of the Balliol and the Bruce families. Additionally, it is important to consider the role of Edward I before and during the Great Cause.

The discussion in this chapter will be divided into the following areas:

- 1.1 The succession problem
- 1.2 The Guardians
- 1.3 The Treaty of Birgham
- 1.4 The death of Margaret the Maid of Norway
- 1.5 The Scottish appeal to Edward I – the decision at Norham
- 1.6 Bruce versus Balliol
- 1.7 The Great Cause and Edward I's decision

1.1 The succession problem

On 19 March 1286 Alexander III was found on the beach under the cliffs at Kinghorn in Fife, his neck broken. The night before, against the better advice of his court nobles, Alexander had travelled in poor conditions from his court in Edinburgh to visit his young wife, Yolande of Dreux, in Fife. It is thought that at some point during the journey he was separated from his party, went missing and fell from his horse. Alexander was found dead the next morning. This started the chain of events leading to the succession crisis in Scotland because Alexander died with no living male heir to the throne. His children from his first marriage had died before him – Alexander (1284), David (1281) and Margaret (1283) – and his wife, Yolande, had not yet given birth. This meant that there was no surviving male heir following the male line of succession and so Scotland entered a brief political crisis until the Guardians were elected.

Prior to his death, Alexander had tried to prevent a situation in which there was no male heir to the throne. Ten years after the death of his first wife, Margaret, and the year after the death of his last son, Alexander, he married Queen Yolande with the intention of having another son to continue his bloodline. When Alexander III died, Yolande was already pregnant. Leading Scottish noble families waited in anticipation for the baby to be born, as the child would be the heir to the now vacant throne. Political leaders, known as the Guardians, gathered at Clackmannanshire to witness the birth in November 1286. However, the child was stillborn. This was an important part of the succession crisis because, when news of the stillborn child circulated, it caused tension within some elements of the political community. As the last hope of a male heir had been lost, the political rulers of Scotland were faced with a difficult question: who should be the next King of Scotland?

Figure 1.1 This image shows the inauguration of King Alexander III on the Moot Hill, Scone. From manuscript of the *Scotichronicon* by Walter Bower, written in *c.*1440. Alexander III ruled Scotland during its golden age, and when he died, Scotland was left without a monarch for many years.

1.2 The Guardians

In the interim period between Alexander III's death in March and the end of Yolande's pregnancy in November, a group of Guardians was chosen. This was a council selected to govern the country and continue the monarchy until an heir could be determined and placed on the throne. The first group of Guardians were elected by the nobility of Scotland in a parliament at Scone on 28 or 29 April 1286. In the absence of a King these men essentially governed Scotland until 1291.

Figure 1.2 This is a cast of the seal of the Guardians of Scotland. On one side it depicts St Andrew, the patron saint of Scotland. The writing around the edge reads: 'Saint Andrew be the leader of the compatriot Scots'. On the other side it shows the lion rampant, symbol of the Scottish crown, with the writing: 'the seal of Scotland appointed for the government of the kingdom'. Royal seals were special because they were double-sided. Unlike normal seals, they had a picture on each side to show off different sides of the monarch's personality. The seal mould was destroyed on 11 June 1291 when the Guardians resigned and were reappointed by Edward I.

These Guardians were 'appointed by and governed in the name of the community of the realm'. In other words, they were chosen by the nobility (their peers) and were charged with ruling Scotland for the benefit of the whole rather than to advance their personal agendas. This was particularly relevant in terms of political crisis as the interests of powerful families were often in competition, and without this legitimacy Scotland could descend into war.

The men chosen were: William Fraser, the **Bishop** of St Andrews; Robert Wishart, Bishop of Glasgow; Duncan, **Earl** of Fife; Alexander Comyn, Earl of Buchan; James Stewart, 5th High Steward; John Comyn of Badenoch; and recently historians have discovered the presence of a seventh Guardian, Bishop William of Dunkeld. These men were deemed the most politically and socially important in Scottish society. The Guardians were to be peacekeeping caretakers, tasked with running the kingdom until the new monarch was enthroned.

Aside from giving away royal land and granting inherited titles, the Guardians collectively shared the powers that the King had exercised. This was an important part of the succession crisis because the Guardians were tasked with protecting the 'community of the realm' in the absence of the King. The Guardians ran Scotland highly effectively on their own from mid-1286 until Edward I's overlordship was acknowledged in June 1291 and their **seal** was broken. After 1291 they governed under Edward I's authority as his appointees.

Although the Guardians were effective in their ruling of Scotland, there were some problems inherent in the Guardians' rule. For example, Guardians William Fraser, Alexander Comyn and John Comyn of Badenoch all had political ties to John Balliol and the Comyn family, whereas Robert Wishart and James Stewart were more politically aligned with the Bruces, another powerful Scottish family. Moreover, the Guardians were not replaced when they died. This meant that when there was an even number of Guardians alive, it would be harder for them to reach collective decisions. Finally, the Guardians were meant to be 'caretakers' until the next monarch was enthroned. Their powers were extensive, but they did not have the same political authority as a King. Therefore, while there is no doubt the Guardians were highly effective in their rule, and governed in the name of the community of the realm, it was known that they could not be a permanent feature and they did not remove political instability in the same way an enthroned monarch would have.

1.3 The Treaty of Birgham

In 1284, after the death of his son Alexander, Alexander III had named his granddaughter, Margaret the Maid of Norway, as his heir were he to die childless. The Maid of Norway was the daughter of King Eric of Norway and Alexander's daughter, Margaret. Naming her as heir was done to give the greatest chance for the continuation of the line of succession, particularly important given the death of his sons. To name a female heir was unusual as it was more common at the time for rulers to be male. Alexander III had hoped that naming the Maid of Norway next in line to the throne would mean that if he died without a male heir, there was a good chance she would be allowed to become Queen. Then, when she married, her husband would rule with her and together they would have more children, which would secure his lineage.

Alexander III held a parliament at Scone in 1284 where the nobles and bishops of Scotland sealed a treaty acknowledging that Margaret the Maid of Norway would be the next in line to the throne. Honouring their **oath** after Alexander III's death in 1286 and Yolande's stillbirth, the Guardians referred to Margaret as 'heir' or 'lady' and began the process of installing her as Queen to maintain peace and avoid further political issues.

The Guardians, Edward I of England and Eric of Norway began negotiations to have Margaret travel to Scotland from her home in Norway. Discussions between Scotland, England and Norway resulted in the Treaty of Salisbury and the Treaty of Birgham. These treaties should have secured Scottish independence and returned the heir to the Scottish throne back to Britain. This would have moved the political challenge caused by Alexander III's death away from who should succeed him, and on to the next phase: governing while the monarch was underage.

As Margaret was only three or four years old when Alexander died, she could have lived in Norway for several years until she was able to rule Scotland herself. However, Eric of Norway, keen for his daughter to sit on the Scottish throne, sent an envoy to Edward I around 21 September 1286, asking him for a loan of up to £2,000. He asked for this because the Scots had not paid the £700 annual **dowry** to Margaret's mother, Margaret, for four years. Edward I put pressure on the Guardians to pay Eric back and, in return, gained a say in her future. This was an important factor in the succession crisis as Edward I's funding enabled the negotiations to bring Margaret to Scotland, with Edward acting as arbiter between Scotland and Norway. The financial and diplomatic contribution made by Edward gave him an important position in deciding what would happen to the Scottish throne. Edward and Eric were discussing this as parents, so there was no necessity for them to involve the Guardians except to make sure the Guardians would hand over the kingdom to the couple. The Guardians' negotiating position was weak because it was difficult for them to justify a refusal of the legitimate heir of Alexander III whom they had already acknowledged. This gave them less control over Scottish affairs and added to the crisis. Edward and Eric used the Guardians' weak bargaining position very skilfully to their own advantage.

The consequence of negotiations was the Treaty of Salisbury, which was concluded on 6 November 1289. The treaty stated that Margaret was to travel from Norway to either Scotland or England by 1 November 1290. She was not to have any marriage contracts and was to make her way from Scotland to England and live with Edward I. A.A.M. Duncan suggests that all three kingdoms were identified in the treaty with an appreciation that when Margaret sailed she would most likely land in Scottish waters, before going south. The treaty ensured the Guardians provided promises that Scotland would remain peaceful and that Edward would send Margaret back up to Scotland when she was old enough without marrying her to anyone in England. Then, if she were to be married, both Edward and Eric of Norway should approve the match. Edward would provide £2,000 for the unpaid dowry that Eric of Norway demanded to facilitate this treaty. All of this was highly significant, as it meant Edward would have leverage over the future heir to the throne of Scotland and so could increase his own power in Scotland. Paying such a huge sum to secure Margaret's arrival in England perhaps reveals Edward's intention to become increasingly involved in Scottish affairs.

SOURCE 1

The King of England has promised that if the lady comes free of all contracts of marriage, when the kingdom of Scotland is in good and secure peace he will be required by the good men of Scotland to send her to the kingdom of Scotland, also free of all contracts of marriage, just as he received her, under the condition that the good people of Scotland make sufficient promises to the King of England ... that they will not marry her without his order, desire and advice, nor without the approval of the King of Norway, her father.

From the Treaty of Salisbury. This was agreed between Edward I, King Eric of Norway and the Scottish Guardians on 6 November 1289 and confirmed by an assembly of 106 Scots at Birgham on 14 March 1290.

The Guardians agreed to the Treaty of Salisbury because they were not in a position to pay Eric of Norway the money that he was demanding for the dowry and because he made comments about concerns over the turbulence of Scottish political life, which could have prevented Margaret's return to Scotland (although it is likely these comments were exaggerated to try to push the case for his daughter coming back as Queen). Therefore, the Guardians agreed to the treaty as it meant that Margaret would be brought to the British Isles more quickly and peacefully, and that they overwhelmingly kept control of their domestic political affairs. However, it arguably added to a growing succession crisis as this choice gave Edward I more authority in Scotland's domestic affairs and in deciding the next King or Queen.

Indeed, ten days later, on 11 November 1289, a **papal bull** was received that stipulated the Pope's approval of the marriage between Margaret and Edward II, Edward I's son. Edward I would have requested this before any documentation was signed with Eric. According to **canon law**, children could not be engaged to be married until they were 7. Although Margaret was 7 at this time, Edward II was not. Marriage normally did not happen until the girl was at least 12 and the boy at least 14. The bull also permitted a marriage but did not contract one. A.A.M. Duncan argues that it was the general understanding and agreement between the negotiating parties that, although Margaret would come to Britain unbetrothed, she would eventually marry Edward II. However, this shows how a crisis was developing as Edward I's choice to seek a papal bull reveals he was intent on bringing Scotland under his control. The marriage of his son to the Scottish heir meant that Scotland and England would be ruled by one monarch, similar to Edward I's land of Aquitaine in France.

In April 1290, the Guardians sent envoys to Edward I seeking guarantees of Scottish independence if, in light of the papal bull, Margaret married Edward II. This led to an agreement between the Guardians and Edward I's envoys at Birgham on 18 July 1290: a document which has become known as the Birgham letter, or the Treaty of Birgham. One clause stated that if Margaret married Edward II, Scotland would remain an independent kingdom with its rights, customs and laws preserved and maintained. For example, Scotland would continue to have an independent **chancellor** and would run its own parliament. If they married, both Edward II and Margaret would have to swear an oath to 'govern the country according to the laws and customs of the land' and that Scotland was 'free in itself, and without subjection from the kingdom of England, as has been observed heretofore'. This is highly significant as it demonstrated that Edward I, by agreeing to this on 28 August 1290, was recognising Scotland's independence. He went this far to ensure that he would gain political control over Scotland through the royal marriage for his son Edward II. This would not be the same as governing Scotland directly, but Margaret and Edward II would have followed English interests diplomatically and the threat of France allying with Scotland against England would have been removed.

On 28 August 1290, Edward I took an unusual step and appointed Bishop Bek as the 'lieutenant' for Margaret and the young Edward II. The other Guardians were told they should listen to Bek in all matters. In other words, Bek was to become the lead Guardian. Edward I's (politically charged) argument for this was that Bek would help keep peace and tranquillity in Scotland. This was a huge shock to the Guardians. Although the proposal identified that 'someone could be appointed to receive clerical election, receive **homages** and **fealties** in place of Margaret before she came of age', to appoint a lead Guardian in this manner was unprecedented. Again, this was perhaps an expression of Edward I's intention in Scotland. However, there is no evidence of the Guardians' reaction and this Guardianship did not go ahead due to later events. G.W.S. Barrow argues that:

> **SOURCE 2**
>
> Even before the Maid of Norway's death it appears that Edward I had set his mind against a voluntary and gradual progress towards union and was contemplating unilateral action. A mere six months after her death he was fully committed to a policy of imposing his authority upon the Scots by force, though without as yet abolishing the kingdom.
>
> **G.W.S. Barrow, 'A kingdom in crisis: Scotland and the Maid of Norway', *The Scottish Historical Review*, Vol. 69, No. 188, Part 2: Studies Commemorative of the Anniversary of the Death of the Maid of Norway (October 1990), 136.**

Edward I had demanded that, before the marriage, Scottish castles were turned over to him for safekeeping, exaggerating claims he was worried that peace in the kingdom would not be maintained without his help. The Guardians refused this but conceded on 28 August 1290 that, instead, they would surrender the castles Edward I wanted to Margaret the Maid of Norway and Edward II when Margaret landed in Scotland. From then on, they would refer to and obey Margaret and Edward II as their 'lady and lord'.

The importance of this clause in the growing political problems cannot be underestimated as it essentially gave possession of parts of Scotland to Edward I through his son. A.A.M. Duncan suggests that this had probably been Edward I's plan since the beginning of the negotiations for the return of Margaret. Although the Guardians stuck to their refusal of giving the land directly to Edward I, as they claimed it was something only a monarch could do, the demands reveal Edward I's intentions and the concessions point to a continuing crisis in Scotland in the future. Moreover, the confusing nature of the wording in this agreement would be used later by both Edward and the Guardians to justify their own positions.

One of the most important clauses was that only when Margaret and Edward II were married and had an heir would the symbols of Scottish **sovereignty**, such as Charters and Relics, the holy rood of St Margaret and the Stone of Destiny, be kept in Scotland. When Margaret was **inaugurated**, a new seal would be created, but it would only be for the Queen of Scots, not a joint seal for wife and husband, making it clear Scotland and England remained separate. This would change when she was married and had come back to Scotland with her husband, at which time the seal would also include her husband, who would be the King. In other words, all the legal and cultural symbols would be maintained for Scotland, an important spiritual and legal statement about its independence as a nation. This should have ended any concern in Scotland about the continuing independence of the nation.

However, news of Margaret's death came a few days later, around 26 September, and thus these discussions, which came to be known as the 'Treaty of Birgham', were never ratified. In fact no Treaty of Birgham ever existed. Edward I argued that, since there had been no ratified treaty as there had been no marriage, there was no legally binding acknowledgement or promise of independence. During discussions, there was no official promise of marriage, no date and no dowry, as would be expected in a treaty. According to canon law, as it was not **ratified**, it was not a treaty and so its claims of Scottish independence were not binding. Conversely, the Guardians felt differently as Edward I had given a written promise to recognise Scottish independence, which did not expressly stipulate that its claims were only valid through marriage. Disputes over the status of what was negotiated at Birgham on 14 July, and agreed in writing by Edward I on 28 April 1290, would inform the rest of the political crisis about overlordship and the succession crisis.

1.4 The death of Margaret the Maid of Norway

As discussed, Margaret the Maid of Norway was Alexander III's only living descendant. She was his granddaughter by his late daughter, Margaret, and the King of Norway, Eric. Although the Guardians had agreed that Margaret the Maid of Norway should be the heir to the throne, this was still a point of contention for the Bruces. There are several reasons why Margaret's position was not favourable.

> **SOURCE 3**
>
> We each and all of us will accept the illustrious girl Margaret as our lady and right heir of our said lord King of Scotland, of the whole realm of Scotland, of the Isle of Man and of all other islands belonging to the said kingdom of Scotland. We will keep and defend her against anyone [who might threaten her] with all our strength and power.
>
> **These words are from the Agreement of Scone, sealed by the 13 earls and 24 other barons of the realm of Scotland in 1284. Seals were flat, round pieces of wax that were used instead of signatures as most people could not write. Nobles had members of the clergy write up their documents for them and then attached their personal seal to show the reader of the document that it was from them. Wax was melted down and stamped with a personal design, before hardening onto the piece of parchment. Because it was extremely difficult to copy someone else's design, seals were very important for recognising whom a document was from and spotting fake documents.**

As a woman in medieval Scotland, Margaret would have been expected to marry a man and not reign herself. The Guardians only refer to her as 'lady' or 'heir', unless in documentation to Edward I, and A.A.M. Duncan argues that it therefore seemed the Guardians were unwilling to acknowledge a female reigning on her own. Typically, **betrothals** were made quickly so as to secure stability. When choosing Margaret's future husband, King Eric of Norway would have to consider both internal and international politics to secure peace in Scotland. This worsened the developing political issues in Scotland, as it made it likely that the influence of other international powers and politics would affect the succession of Scotland's royal family.

Margaret's sex and age precluded her from leading an army into battle. She could not be depicted in armour or on horseback on her seal and so could only have a coat of arms. She was only seven (in 1290) and would not be able to contribute to politics for many years. This was an issue because statesmanship and military campaigning were important parts of the role of medieval monarchs and helped them seem legitimate in the eyes of their nobility as they added land and wealth to the country. Bravery and valour on the battlefield were highly respected qualities and monarchs who did not demonstrate them were considered weak and were vulnerable to expulsion. After Alexander III's death, it is clear that the Guardians were in no hurry to return Margaret to Scotland, as they were able to run the country in her absence and on her behalf. This avoided the instability that would be created by a young and female monarch.

Scotland had no history of a female monarch. Medieval Scotland was a highly patriarchal society and so, as the first Queen of Scotland, Margaret would have had to operate in a system where it was normal for women to be considered secondary and women were expected to obey their husbands. This had the consequence that her nobles and political community would not automatically take her decisions seriously, undermining her political authority and the stability of the realm.

Finally, historians agree that the Guardians would have been aware that the Queen might not survive to adulthood. Child mortality was high in medieval Europe and there was no guarantee she would live long enough to marry and produce an heir to the throne. If she died before reaching her **majority**, Scotland would once again be left without a clear heir to the throne. So, it is clear that although Margaret was the heir, her **minority** rule would have posed many security and political risks, which meant that some thought she should be replaced by an adult male.

However, many of these problems did not materialise, as Margaret never reached Scotland. She set sail for Scotland from Norway in September 1290. However, her boat was caught in a storm and anchored in Orkney. There, she died. Her death brought an end to Alexander III's line, the House of Canmore, which had occupied the Scottish throne since 1058. It also marked the end of the negotiations that would have led to a Treaty of Birgham between the Guardians of Scotland and Edward I of England. Her death created a new political situation in Scotland – a real succession crisis. Scotland was once again without a ruling monarch, but this time there was no clear way to identify who would be the next ruler.

On Margaret's death, Bishop Fraser informed Edward I that Robert Bruce V (grandfather of Robert Bruce VII) and the Earls of Atholl and Mar were planning on taking power. Fraser asked Edward I for assistance in stopping a civil war. Without a ruling monarch or an heir to the throne, Scotland was vulnerable to domestic unrest as different groups laid their claims to the throne.

Bruce V was one of the men who felt that he should be King instead of Margaret. He also had a claim to the throne, which will be discussed in the next chapter. However, with Margaret's death, Bruce and his followers also appealed to Edward I in the 'Appeal of the Seven Earls', which asked Edward I to support Bruce's claim to the throne. These two letters demonstrate that Scotland was on the brink of civil war.

1.5 The Scottish appeal to Edward I – the decision at Norham

The death of Margaret the Maid of Norway brought the political problems of the previous four years to a head. Powerful **claimants** to the throne were active in asserting the legitimacy of their claims, and the political situation was becoming so tense that key contemporaries believed a costly civil war was on the horizon. Robert Bruce V, who was grandfather to the future King of Scots (see Figure 1.5 on page 16), and his allies were co-operating to install him as King. At the same time, the Comyn–Balliol family had strengthened its political influence over Scotland. On the news of Margaret's death, both parties appealed to Edward I to support their own claims to the throne of Scotland. This led to Edward I being asked to arbitrate in what is called the 'Great Cause' to determine the next rightful King of Scots.

The first appeal was by Bruce V and his followers, sometime between 1290 and 1291, in the 'Appeal of the Seven Earls'. The appeal, in the form of a letter, stated that the Guardians Bishop Fraser and John Comyn of Badenoch were colluding to make John Balliol King to strengthen their own power in Scotland. The appeal accused Fraser and Badenoch of pillaging royal lands in Moray, according to a complaint from the Earl of Mar, causing significant loss of life. It also accused them of dominating Scottish politics since the death of Alexander III. Most significantly, the letter requested that Edward I support Bruce's claim to the throne. This was an important political document because, although its claims about Fraser and Comyn may have been somewhat exaggerated, it suggests the Scottish nobility was politically divided over who should be King. The Bruce faction were active in pressing their claim from October 1290 onwards, despite the rule of the Guardians.

The second appeal was made by Bishop Fraser in response to Bruce V's vocal ambitions to be King. Fraser wrote to Edward I in October 1290 claiming that when the news of Margaret's death was announced, Bruce unexpectedly arrived in Perth and aggressively reasserted his claim to be King. Unlike his brief uprising in 1286, which was limited to the south-west, the disturbance in October 1290 was national, not regional, in its significance. Bishop Fraser asked Edward to step in and decide the new King of Scots to prevent civil war. Historians debate whether this letter was trying to persuade Edward to make Balliol King or just prevent civil war. Fraser would have been well aware of Balliol's close ties to England and, although there is evidence he was pro-Comyn, that did not automatically mean he was pro-Balliol. The long record of Balliol's ties to Edward's throne mean it can be argued that Fraser may have been worried that Balliol would run Scotland as a **vassal kingdom** to England – and specifically that the independence of the Scottish Church would be called into question. This was important as Fraser contacted Edward without the knowledge of the other Guardians, demonstrating the cracks in the temporary government of Scotland and the crisis this created from October 1290 onwards. These appeals demonstrate the political significance of Margaret's death, and the instability it caused in the succession crisis.

Another problem was that if Fraser did support Balliol, then his appeal should be interpreted as asking the English King to install him as the new King of Scots, and giving Edward I strong assurances that there was a community in Scotland (the Comyns) that would support his claim. If this was the case, it demonstrates that neither side had managed to gain enough support in Scotland to secure the kingship by force, as there was no other accepted political or legal procedure for determining who should be King. Both of these letters asked for the English King's help in deciding Scottish affairs, demonstrating the complicated political nature of the succession crisis.

There were a number of reasons why Edward I was asked to help decide the future monarch. First, England was Scotland's closest neighbour and under Alexander III's rule the two countries had co-existed peacefully. Edward was the brother-in-law of Alexander III and so uncle to Margaret the Maid of Norway: there was no obvious reason not to ask him to intervene. These ties of family meant that Edward had worked with Alexander III before and the Guardians assumed this would continue. He had also been critical in securing Scotland after Alexander III's death: in organising the negotiations for the Treaty of Birgham/Salisbury which would have ensured that Margaret returned to Scotland. Moreover, many Scottish lords held land in England so were already **vassals** of both realms. They were called 'cross-border lords'. So, politically, it made sense to call on Edward to arbitrate over the crucial decision of who should be the next King since the pair would share many of the same subjects. Edward was an experienced statesman, crusader and conqueror of Wales: well versed in legal matters and renowned for his fairness in legal disputes. All of this meant that it was unlikely anyone would dispute his choice, hopefully preventing any further political unrest in Scotland.

To decide which laws and customs should be applied and help judge the claimants, Edward I sought expert legal advice from Oxford and Cambridge and from overseas. This implied that he wanted to make an informed decision and one that was internationally respected. Despite his offers of help, in early 1291 Edward ordered a search of the government rolls and monastic libraries in England to find evidence of a historic claim of English overlordship of Scotland. It was clear he was intending to make Scotland a vassal to England, or at least exert some form of political control. This would cause a huge crisis, as the point of asking Edward in the first place had been to ensure Scottish independence, not allow it to become an extension of England. Instead, Edward insisted that he should be judged as overlord.

Edward I first met with the Scottish Guardians between 10 May and 12 June 1291. The Guardians met at Upsettlington, on the north and Scottish side of the River Tweed, whereas Edward and his men came only as far as Norham Castle on the English side of the river. Edward refused to cross the border and demanded that the Guardians came to him. This was taken as both insulting and unusual by some at the time, as it meant the process of finding a new King for Scotland would start on English soil. However, the Guardians had little choice so met Edward at Norham. This was partly because in June 1291 Edward had placed an intimidatingly large force of 1,300 men and a fleet of ships on the border of Scotland. This was certainly a reminder of the strength of the English state and an encouragement to comply with his demands. This was highly damning as it demonstrated that Edward would be prepared to use force and be aggressive to strengthen his own position in relation to the Guardians during negotiations. It suggests he was keen to assert dominance during this period of political turmoil in Scotland, contributing to the succession crisis.

At Norham, Edward I insisted on personally judging the Great Cause rather than arbitrating as a friendly neighbour, as he had originally been asked to do. He demanded that the Guardians swear an oath of loyalty to him before he would choose the next King, in effect making him **overlord** of Scotland. This took the Guardians by surprise and arguably foreshadowed Edward's intentions in Scotland. In response to this, on 2 June, the Bishop of Glasgow replied to Edward claiming that they did not know about Edward's right to have overlordship and, even if they did, that only the King of Scots could reply to such a demand. Since there was no King at present, they had no power to swear such an oath. It is clear that the succession crisis in Scotland had intensified significantly, as the lack of an anointed King put the future of Scottish independence in jeopardy. So, in short, the succession crisis was becoming a crisis of independence.

Edward I instead demanded that all 13 claimants to the throne swore loyalty to him and agreed to his overlordship. Fearing that they would be left out of the judgement, 9 of the claimants accepted Edward's overlordship. In doing so, they gave up the independence of the kingdom. Interestingly, Robert Bruce V was first to swear the oath, while Balliol was last. The decision to promise Edward the position of overlord is known as the Award of Norham. This demonstrates that the succession crisis had intensified dramatically, as with this oath Edward had the legal power to control Scotland and give away parts of the land, and Scotland's new King would be subservient to him. This had not been the case in Scotland in living memory.

Historians suggest that the fact that Balliol was the last to swear an oath of loyalty to Edward I and was delayed in making that oath could be because Edward I had already agreed with Balliol that he would be named as King, and so he needed to wait for his fealty before the court at Berwick could continue. This suggests that Edward was not as transparent about his decision as he appeared.

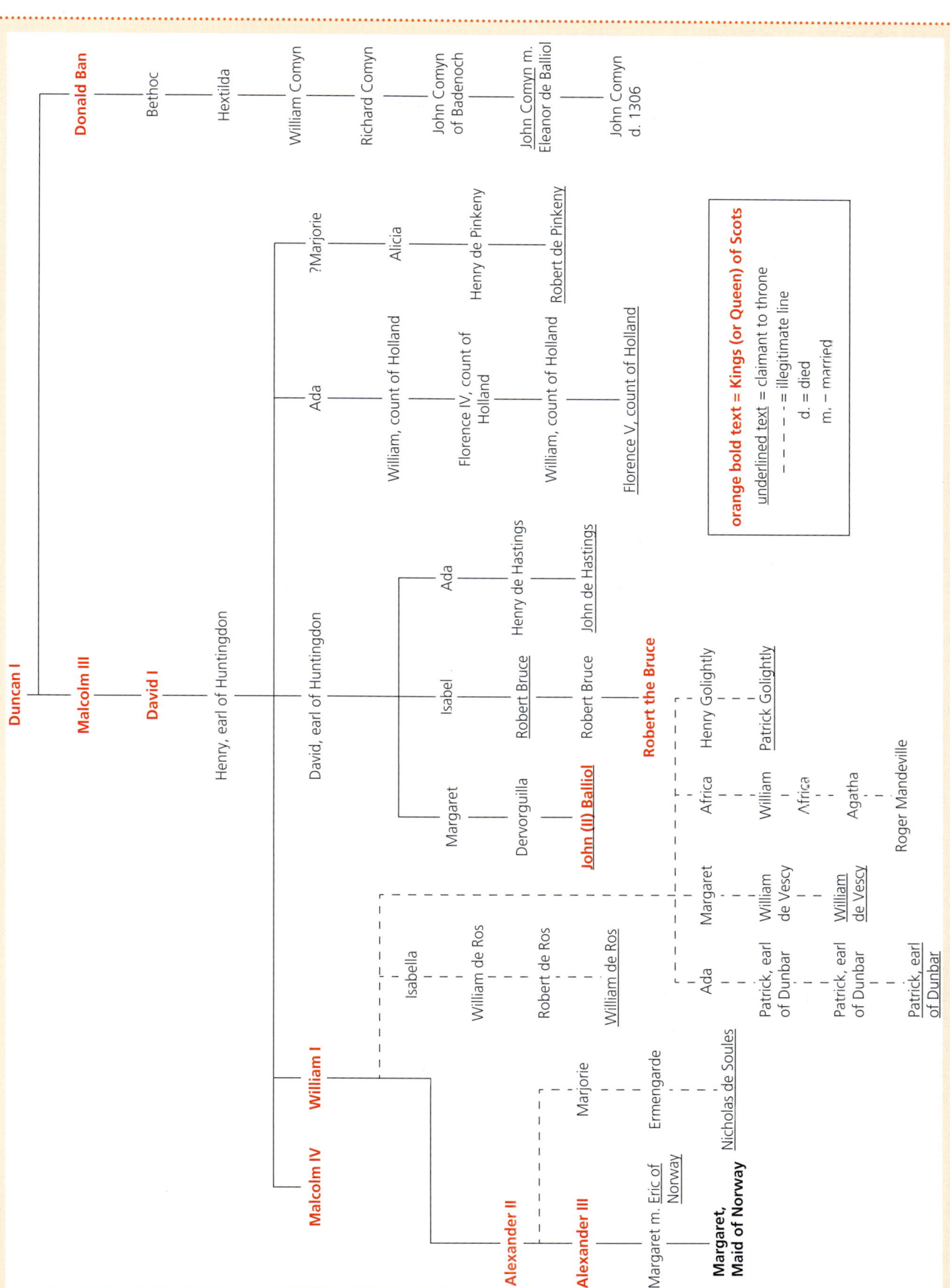

Figure 1.3 Family tree of the 13 claimants to the throne of Scotland, 1290–92.

1.6 Bruce versus Balliol

A significant element of the succession crisis was the competition between powerful Scottish families. Two of the most important families involved were the Bruces and the Balliols. These families clashed throughout this period as they advanced their competing claims to inherit the throne of Scotland. This section details the competition of the Bruces and Balliols, from the time of Alexander III's death in 1286 until the Award of Norham in 1291.

Robert Bruce V had a claim to the throne through his mother Isabel's line of descent. She was the second daughter of David, Earl of Huntingdon (d. 1219), who in turn was the youngest grandson of David I of Scotland (d. 1153). Similarly, John Balliol (II) had a claim through the female line of his descent. His mother was the daughter of Margaret, David Earl of Huntingdon's eldest daughter. However, his mother, Dervorguilla of Galloway (Derb Forgaill in the medieval Gaelic spelling), was still alive and active in Scotland's political and social life and so he did not inherit his claim until after her death in 1290. Hence from this time onwards these two men (Bruce and Balliol) had competing and strong claims to the throne – and this competition caused political instability.

Bruce V and Balliol were each a senior representative of the competing branches of the old ruling families of Galloway. Although Balliol's whereabouts between 1286 and 1290 are unknown, there was little point him pursuing his claim while his mother and Margaret the Maid of Norway survived, as they had a claim through the female line before he did. This did, however, contribute to the succession crisis as Balliol was allied to the Comyns, the most powerful family in Scotland, through the marriage of John Balliol's sister Eleanor to John Comyn in 1270. Balliol left Scottish politics to be dominated by the Comyn faction, who promoted his interests in the hope that, if Margaret died, their allegiance would result in their retaining significant power in Scotland. Therefore, Balliol's claim to the throne added to the political instability in Scotland, as the Comyn family pushed to support his claim.

There is evidence that John Balliol had ties to Edward I. He spent some time as a ward of Edward's court in his youth and married Isabella de Warenne around 9 February 1281. Isabella was the daughter of John de Warenne, Earl of Surrey and Edward's cousin. The marriage certainly secured kinship ties between the two families and resulted in Edward helping the Balliols out of some significant inherited family debt in the mid-1280s. According to the Yorkshire Chronicle of Meaux, John Balliol made Edward godfather to his son, Edward Balliol. Scotland, as with all of Europe, was a deeply religious society and so this created a social and spiritual tie between the families, known at the time as 'kinship', which applied to blood marriage ties. As godfather, Edward was expected to help Edward Balliol if he was in need or risked facing **damnation** in **purgatory**. This arguably contributed to the succession crisis as the Balliol family had enough political importance, lands in England and Scotland, and a strong enough claim to the Scottish succession, that Edward intervened in their affairs.

Although it is hard to date precisely when the Bruce family made its first claim to the throne, Robert Bruce V recollected that Alexander II had recognised him as heir before Alexander III died – although there is no document to prove this. Similarly, there is no document to suggest Bruce made a claim while Alexander III was alive. There is no evidence of John Balliol's engagement in Scottish politics during Alexander III's reign, aside from his presence at Scone in 1284. So, it can be argued that the succession crisis was not inevitable upon Alexander III's death.

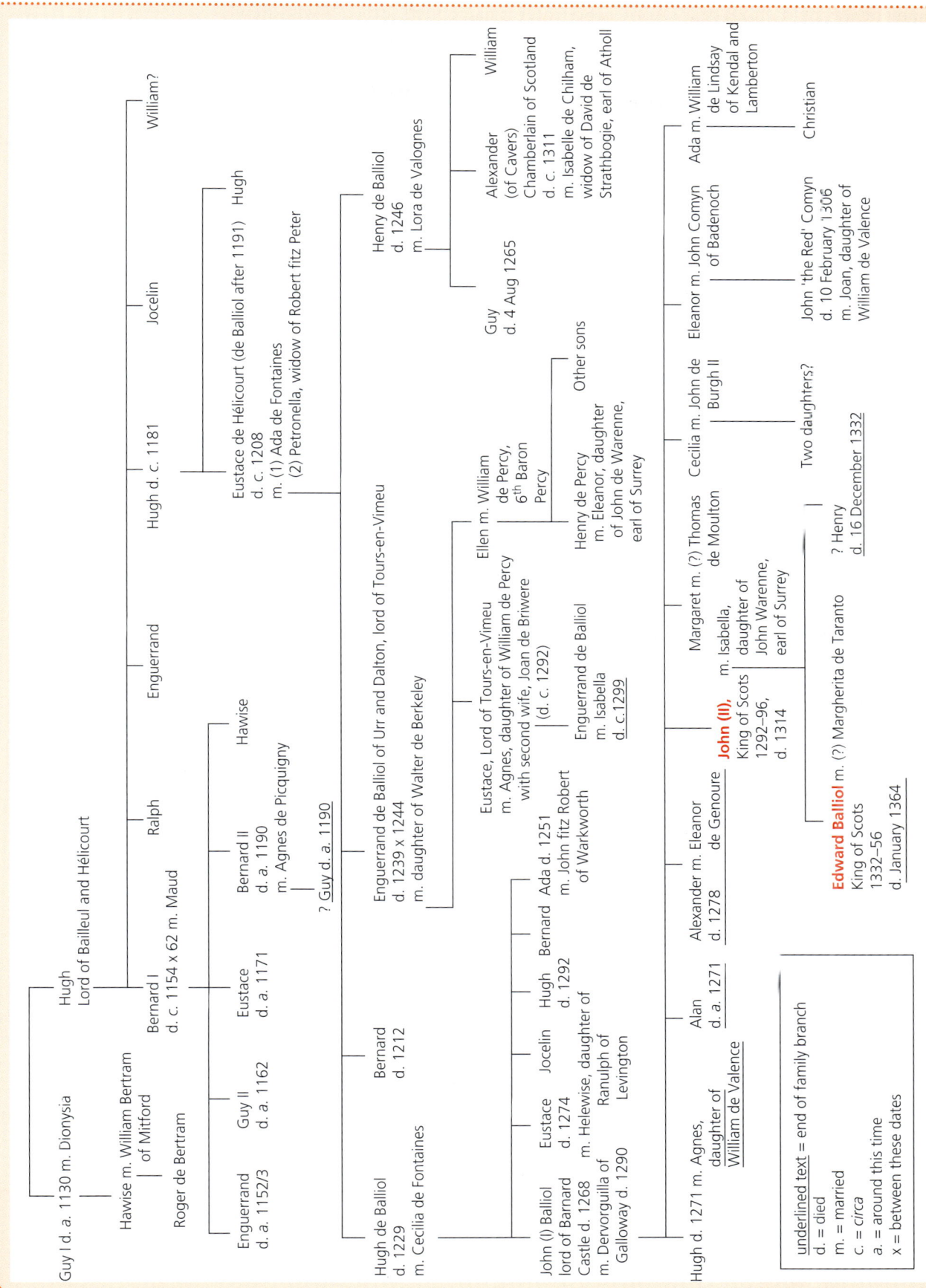

Figure 1.4 The Balliol family tree showing the line of descent to John Balliol, who would become King John I of Scotland.

A parliament was held on 28 or 29 April 1286. After it had ended, Bruce V withdrew to Carrick to gather an army in the winter of 1286, after Yolande's baby was pronounced stillborn. He launched attacks on Balliol castles in the south-west with such violence and destruction that there was no income from destroyed lands of Dumfries and Wigtown for two years after the conflict. The fighting was successfully subdued later that winter by the Guardians. However, the Bruces had gathered enough political support in Scotland to protect themselves from exile and so were able to reassert their claim for the throne in October 1290.

Bruce V continued to gather support in Scotland. The 'Turnberry Band' was signed on 20 September 1286. This was a pact signed at Turnberry Castle, the seat of the Bruces, between several important Scottish and Anglo-Irish nobles, including Bruce, swearing an oath to support each other. Notable signatories included the Earl of Dunbar and his three sons, the Earl of Menteith and his two sons, the Guardian James Stewart and the Earl of Ulster, and the Lord of Islay and his son, Alexander Og. This oath agreed mutual support of each other's military endeavours and 'in all their affairs, and with them and their accomplices to stand faithfully in resistance against all their adversaries'. This demonstrated the ability of Robert Bruce V to rouse significant political support in his region. When considering the succession crisis, this should not be underestimated because the knowledge of the Band circulated around Scotland and acted as **propaganda** encouraging others who had rivalries with the Comyns to consider being potential allies of the Bruces. However, this did not work and peace was restored after Bruce's uprising.

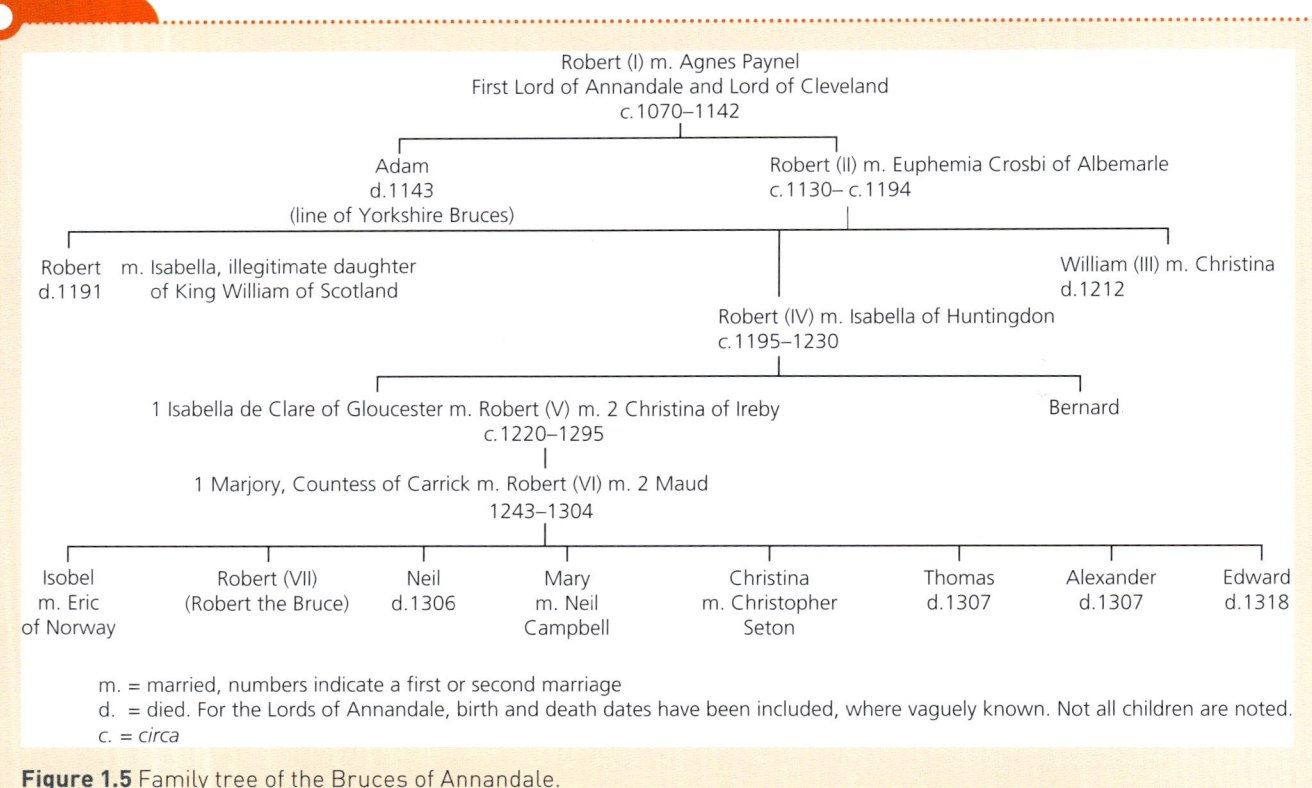

Figure 1.5 Family tree of the Bruces of Annandale.

Balliol also established a close relationship with Bishop Bek of Durham, Edward I's chief representative in Scotland. It had been stated in 1289 by Edward that Bek would be the lieutenant of Margaret the Maid of Norway and her prospective husband, if that husband was Edward II of England. This pro-Edward I connection worried Bishop Fraser who wanted to preserve the independence of the Scottish Church. Having Edward I's bishop intervene in Scottish affairs put the position of the Scottish Church in jeopardy, and thus added to the developing political crisis.

Robert Bruce V continued to press his claim to the throne internationally, across the border in England. He independently reached out to Edward I to promote his claim as King of Scots and made strong political ties across Scotland to strengthen his position. The Appeal of the Seven Earls, discussed above on page 10, asserted Bruce's right to the Scottish throne and demonstrates that he felt he was in a favourable position to acquire the kingship and was willing to work with Edward I to support his claim, even if this meant he conceded some of his power to him.

Bruce V made further political alliances in Scotland between 1287 and 1289 with Donald, Earl of Mar, and John Strathbogie, Earl of Atholl, both powerful members of the nobility, to provide mutual protection for their lands from the Comyns of Buchan and Badenoch. So, although the Bruces' lands were in the south-west, in Carrick and Annandale, between 1286 and 1289 they created a network across Scotland that made them significantly stronger than they had been in 1286, adding to the political threat in Scotland by October 1290.

1.7 The Great Cause and Edward I's decision

The task of choosing a new King for the Scottish throne, known as the Great Cause, was a long drawn-out process of discussion, argument and the presentation of evidence in support of the claimants. Edward I was asked to make the decision about who should be King. Thirteen claimants presented themselves as possible heirs to the throne, although only three, John Balliol, Robert Bruce V and John Hastings, had a strong legal claim. All three were descendants of the daughters of David, Earl of Huntingdon, a descendant of David I of Scotland.

It is important to note that, as mentioned above, Edward I insisted that he should judge this decision as overlord.

The first issue in the Great Cause was identifying an appropriate method to select the next King. Before Margaret the Maid of Norway's death, there had not been, in living memory, a succession crisis which provided precedent for a definitive legal or regal ruling to help establish royal customs about who would be the next ruler. Edward I chose the principle of **primogeniture**, a system of inheritance from father to son, or to son's son, or to brother's nephew, and so on. This was the obvious choice and it is clear that, as primogeniture was chosen, Edward I had selected the method that was legal and traditional. Therefore, the decision would be respected by the Scots, the Church and the international community. However, as the only blood heir was a minor female (now deceased), and with several male heirs coming from more than one generation, primogeniture could not be applied straightforwardly. If there were only female heirs, the custom of primogeniture was to divide the inheritance between each sister or her heirs. The problem was that, because Scotland was a kingdom, it was uncertain that it could simply be divided. So, if the normal rules of primogeniture could not be applied, it was open to question how an alternative arrangement could be justified legally. As a result, the case between Balliol and Bruce was finely balanced in legal terms, adding to the succession crisis.

Edward I's court, held at Berwick, decided to hear the Bruce and Balliol cases, as they were the strongest claimants, and then measure the remaining claims against the winner. Both Bruce and Balliol were asked to supply 40 of their own followers from the nobility to the court to help demonstrate which Scottish nobles were in favour of each claim and to provide evidence to support their respective claims. Although Bruce's men were certainly politically weaker than Balliol's, the split in supporters demonstrates that the political elite of Scotland were not unanimous about who should be the next King. Many were worried that if Balliol took the throne, Scotland would be controlled by the English King. However, Balliol had Comyn support in his following and, as they were the most politically and militarily dominant family in Scotland, this carried significant clout.

It is clear that Edward I was following expected protocol to allow both sides to have their own council. However, he then went on to add his own council to the mix. This was an important action as it asserted his overlordship and helps demonstrate that he planned to act as judge rather than arbiter.

When the first part of the case – deciding which laws should be used – went against Bruce V, and he knew he would lose, he supported the position of another claimant, John Hastings. Hastings' position was that the custom of primogeniture for when there were only female heirs, i.e. to divide the inheritance between each sister or her heirs, should be applied to the kingdom of Scotland. This was to ensure that they each got something rather than nothing. Instead of picking one King, Hastings and Bruce wanted Scotland to be divided between each of the claimants, arguing that it could not possibly be legal to choose between them. This had the potential of contributing to the succession crisis as it meant that the kingdom would be split in three between Balliol, Bruce and Hastings. If this happened, Scotland would cease to exist as a unit of government. It would be a kingdom in name only. This shows just how far Robert Bruce V was willing to go to gain power in Scotland. Although this might have appeased the relative claimants, the fact that Edward I did not choose this method is important. Bruce's method left a high chance that political rivalries would re-emerge between the ruling elites, making the effort to settle the dispute pointless. This might suggest that Edward wanted to find a way to resolve conflict permanently.

There was a long adjournment between August 1291 and June 1292 to allow Count Floris of Holland, one of the claimants, to find documentation proving his claim to the throne. Floris claimed that David, Earl of Huntingdon, had renounced his claim to the throne, which meant that none of his heirs – including Balliol, Bruce and Hastings – could inherit. Floris was descended from Ada, granddaughter of David I, so this document would make him the rightful heir. However, the document, once found, was deemed to be a forgery. Nonetheless, as time dragged on, Edward I capitalised on the delay. He acted as direct lord of Scotland during this period, weakening the country significantly. He toured from Haddington to St Andrews and Stirling, and received oaths of fealty from the Scottish nobility. At each court he made it clear that the claimants had sworn oaths of fealty to English overlordship, destabilising the Scottish realm and adding to the crisis.

Edward I's final judgement was made in favour of John Balliol in November 1292. After much debate, Edward's councillors had agreed that the candidate descended from the younger sister, and the closer male to the throne (Bruce), should not be preferred over one descended from the elder sister (Balliol). Balliol had the strongest legal claim, based on an adapted form of primogeniture as if John Balliol's mother and grandmother had been male rather than female. This decision probably had the support of the majority. Historians suggest that at the time it was widely agreed that Edward's choice to appoint Balliol as King of Scots was legal and fair. John Balliol would be inaugurated King John I of Scots at Scone Palace on 30 November 1292.

> **SOURCE 4**
>
> The King, as overlord of the kingdom of Scotland, after hearing and noting the demands and arguments of John Hastings and Robert Bruce, who were asking for their shares [one-third of the kingdom], and examining them carefully, declares as a matter of law and by way of judgment that the realm of Scotland cannot be split, and that the acquisitions of the kings of Scotland cannot be split either. But the lands outside the realm of Scotland should be dealt with according to the laws and customs of the realms of where they are. Therefore the King declares by way of judgement that you, John Hastings and Robert Bruce, shall receive nothing of the shares which you demand.
>
> But to you, John Balliol, as nearest heir of Margaret, daughter of the King of Norway, lady of Scotland, and grand-daughter of the late Alexander, King of Scotland, by right of succession to the realm of Scotland as determined before the King, the King hands over the realm and possession of it, with all the privileges of the kingdom and those things which have come into the hands of the King as overlord since the death of Margaret, except the right in Scotland of the King and his heirs when they wish to raise the point.
>
> **This is an extract from the judgement delivered by Edward I at Berwick on 17 November 1292 at the end of the legal process (the 'Great Cause') to determine who should succeed after the death of Margaret the Maid of Norway. Edward I's decision about who should be King of Scotland was announced in the hall of Berwick Castle, in front of Edward I, bishops, earls and 80 people who had been elected to hear the claims to the throne.**

1.8 Overall

The events which eventually led to the succession crisis began in Scotland with the death of Alexander III because there was no immediate male heir to the throne. The Guardians were effective rulers and kept the country at peace until Yolande's stillbirth. Although the political crisis seemed to be staved off when Scotland and England agreed to the Treaty of Birgham, which secured Scottish independence and the heir to the throne, the death of Margaret the Maid of Norway invalidated all negotiations. The succession crisis quickly emerged and revealed significant political rivalries in Scotland. The Guardians and some of the nobility turned to Edward I to help identify the next King of Scots. Factionalism between the Bruces, the Balliols and the Comyns continued and Scotland deepened its political divisions. Finally, after 18 months of deliberation, Edward I chose John Balliol as King of Scots because he was the nearest male heir through the eldest female line of descent. Throughout this period, Edward I demonstrated that he wanted to gain more power in Scotland.

By 1292, John Balliol was John I, King of Scots. Edward I of England was Scotland's overlord. John I began his rule after Scotland had been weakened by years of political instability as a result of the protracted succession crisis.

ACTIVITIES

1. Part of understanding this topic is understanding why there was a succession crisis in Scotland. Cut out ten arrows, like the one below, from paper or card. Now, cut up ten rectangles, as below. Follow the instructions:
   a. From this chapter, select ten events and people that you think helped to make the succession crisis in Scotland worse between 1286 and 1292.
   b. In the arrows, draw an image to represent each event/person.
   c. In the rectangles, write a one-sentence explanation of why the event/person helped eventually to cause a succession crisis. Your sentence should start with 'This helped to cause a succession crisis because…'
   d. Test yourself. Mix your arrows and rectangles up and try to rematch them as quickly as you can.
   e. Now, order your arrow and rectangle pairs from the most important reason there was a succession crisis to the least important.
   f. Explain why there was a succession crisis in Scotland in four sentences.

2. Key to understanding this topic is understanding the role of Edward I. Follow the instructions:
   a. Make a list of all the actions of Edward I between 1286 and 1292 leading up to and during the succession crisis.
   b. Rank these into 'actions that promoted Scotland's independence' and 'actions that worked against Scotland's independence'.
   c. Using what you have found, summarise his role in one sentence.
   d. Make a set of at least ten quiz questions about the role of Edward I between 1286 and 1292.

3. Higher source handling requires knowledge and explanation of causes, events and impacts of different historical events. Use the information in this chapter to make a mind map with at least ten points explaining the causes of the succession crisis in Scotland. Include at least one detailed fact and use the word 'because' in each point to explain your answer.

GLOSSARY

Term	Meaning
baron	The lord of a local area who not only controls the land but has his own law court to enforce the law over the inhabitants.
betrothal	Formal engagement to be married; engagement.
bishop	A senior member of the Christian clergy who has authority over priests in local churches within a region (known as a 'diocese'). He controls the behaviour of priests and has the authority to make priests and authorise their appointment to a local church.
canon law	Ecclesiastical law, especially (in the Roman Catholic Church) that laid down by papal pronouncements.
chancellor	The senior legal official in royal government who controls the royal seal and authorises government documents.
claimant	A person who, through a legitimate or illegitimate inheritance, has a claim to a title or position.
damnation	Condemnation to eternal punishment in hell.
dowry (or tocher)	An amount of property or money brought by a bride to her husband on their marriage.
earl	The highest rank of the nobility in medieval Scotland.
fealty	A formal acknowledgement of loyalty to another person, similar to an oath
homage	A ceremony of personal submission to a superior lord.
inaugurate	To enthrone the King or Queen in an official ceremony.
lord	Second highest rank of the nobility in medieval Scotland.
majority	A monarch's personal rule when they are old enough to take charge themselves, without the support of a regent.
minority	When a child is a monarch but is too young to rule the country themselves.
oath	A solemn promise, often invoking a divine witness, regarding one's future action or behaviour.
overlord	A ruler, especially a feudal lord.
papal bull	A formal document issued by a Pope.
parliament	'Parliament' was initially only one of a number of words to refer to an assembly of prominent men summoned by the King to pass laws, settle disputes and provide advice to the King. It became more formal during Alexander III's reign, requiring the summons to be made 40 days before it met. By 1286 'parliament' had become the regular term for these assemblies.
primogeniture	The right of succession belonging to the firstborn son (or their son, down the male line). If there are daughters instead of sons, the lands are divided between them.
propaganda	Information, especially of a biased or misleading nature, used to promote a political cause or point of view.
purgatory	(In Catholic doctrine) a place or state of suffering inhabited by the souls of sinners who are making amends for their sins before going to heaven.
ratified	To ratify a document or treaty is to seal or give formal consent.
seal	A piece of wax with an individual design stamped into it, attached to a document as a guarantee of authenticity. Important individuals and groups in medieval society had their own seal.
sovereignty	The supreme power or authority of a person or country.
stillborn	A stillbirth is when a baby is born dead after 24 completed weeks of pregnancy.
tenant farmer	A person who farms rented land.
vassal	A holder of land on conditions of homage and allegiance.
vassal kingdom	A kingdom whose King is under the authority of another King. By the time of the Wars of Independence it was expected that a King would be the ultimate authority in his own kingdom (apart from in matters involving religion or canon law). John Balliol's position as King of Scots under the overlordship of Edward I was highly unusual, therefore.

Chapter 2

John Balliol and Edward I, 1292–96

> The aim of this chapter is to evaluate the relationship between John Balliol and Edward I during the reign of Balliol as King John I, and to consider how Scotland was brought under Edward I's control by 1296.

LINK TO EXAM

Higher

Key issue 2: John Balliol and Edward I, 1292–96

Background

John Balliol was enthroned King John I of Scots on 30 November 1292, St Andrew's Day. Balliol was one of 13 claimants for the Scottish crown in the Great Cause (1291–92). He was a great-great-great-grandson of King David I of Scots through his mother, Dervorguilla of Galloway. This meant he was one generation further from David than his main rival, Robert Bruce V, fifth Lord of Annandale (grandfather of Robert Bruce VII, who later became King). However, as his grandmother Margaret was the eldest daughter of Earl David (d. 1219), David I's grandson, he was the senior line in genealogical primogeniture if not by proximity of blood (see Figure 1.4 on page 15).

Figure 2.1 Seal of Dervorguilla of Galloway.

Balliol (King John I) ruled Scotland between 1292 and 1296 with both the help and hindrance of Edward I and the Scottish nobility. Although he would have some success, he was eventually sidelined by the Scottish nobility, and the Franco-Scottish Treaty would result in Edward I conquering Scotland in 1296 and forcing Balliol to abdicate.

Why did Balliol face problems during his reign between 1292 and 1296?

For the exam, it is important to understand the relationship between Balliol and Edward I between 1292 and 1296. To understand this, it is important to consider the problems Balliol faced during his rule, the war with France and the subsequent conquest of Scotland in 1296.

> The factors studied here and relating to the relationship between John Balliol and Edward I 1292–96, including the problems Balliol faced during his rule, are:
> - 2.1 Balliol's rule
> - 2.2 Edward I's overlordship
> - 2.3 The Scottish response
> - 2.4 The Anglo-French War and the Franco-Scottish Treaty
> - 2.5 The subjugation of Scotland, 1296

2.1 Balliol's rule

Historians have been critical of John Balliol's rule in Scotland. However, he faced many issues that made his rule a challenge from the start. He did not have the political education normal for a medieval monarch, he was in debt to Edward I, and the Comyn family dominated his government.

One challenge that Balliol faced was his lack of political experience. Balliol was enthroned King at around 43 years old. As the youngest of four Balliol sons, he would not have expected to inherit or control his family lands, as all lands and titles would have been inherited by the eldest son. However, with the death of his brothers, probably in a crusade or fighting for the English King, he inherited his family lands in 1278 in England at 29 years old. Balliol had little military training. He had also not been highly active in Scottish politics before the 1290s, though it is worth noting that he was one of the barons who assembled at Scone in 1284 and 1286 to recognise Margaret the Maid of Norway as Alexander III's heir. A lack of political or military experience was a problem for Balliol and undermined his rule from the start. He had not had the upbringing and training of a future King and did not understand the inner workings of the Scottish court.

As well as land, Balliol also inherited significant family debt to the English crown from his father and grandfather. Although some of these debts were cancelled or deferred by Edward I, on Balliol's marriage to Isabella and during the Great Cause, Balliol remained in debt to the English King during his reign. Furthermore, Edward I was godfather to John Balliol and Isabella's first son, also named Edward. As godfather, Edward I would have been present at Edward Balliol's christening and the Church would have expected him to support his godson. Finally, Balliol had probably worked as a clerk for the English King before inheriting his estates. It is important to understand these ties of debt, land and **kin** because they put the Balliol family in a position of obligation to the crown of England from the start of Balliol's reign.

Therefore, at the beginning of his rule in Scotland, Balliol may have felt an obligation to comply with Edward I's commands, though it is clear that he often did so only under duress.

There is strong evidence to suggest that Balliol's government was dominated by its most powerful supporters, the Comyn family. The Comyns had been influential in Scottish politics for some time, and had been the strongest political force in Scotland since the death of Alexander six years earlier. The Comyns backed Balliol's claim to the throne. John Comyn the elder joined the ranks of claimants, but this was only after the numbers of claimants swelled: he acted together with Balliol, joining him as the last to submit to Edward I's claim to overlordship in June 1291. Moreover, John Comyn was Balliol's brother-in-law. At Balliol's first parliament as King, at Scone in 1293, he attempted to consolidate his power in Scotland by granting over 20 'ordinances' to gather political support.

On one hand, this is significant because it demonstrates that Balliol was able to wield his power quickly, and understood the importance of consolidating his support in a Scotland that still had significant rivalries between powerful families. It could also be argued that Balliol was wise to accept the help and support of such an experienced and powerful Scottish family as the Comyns, as he realised this would help him consolidate his power in Scotland.

However, a large number of political and land disputes were settled in favour of Balliol's Comyn supporters. For example, the Earl of Ross was appointed sheriff of Skye, Barra, Lewis and Uist instead of the rival MacRuaridh family. Also, MacDougal was appointed sheriff of Argyll and the southern Western Isles instead of the MacDonald family. However, these appointments heightened the disputes between these families. It seems unlikely that, considering Balliol's relative newness to the Scottish political scene, he would have known to which groups to grant land, and therefore political privilege, so quickly. This suggests that the Comyn family were dominant in Balliol's court and that, by overly favouring the Comyns and their interests, Balliol may have been exacerbating regional rivalries within Scotland rather than resolving them.

There is also some evidence that Balliol tried to assert himself as King on an equal footing to Edward I. The wording of the Royal Seal of Scotland was to be changed to follow the formula used by Kings of England on their seal. This suggests that Balliol was keen to assert that his kingship was on the same basis as King Edward's.

2.2 Edward I's overlordship

From the start of Balliol's reign, Edward I intervened heavily in the organisation of the Scottish government. Master Thomas of Hunsingore, who had ties to the Balliols as well as leading English families, advised John. The office of treasurer, which was used in England, was also introduced. It was occupied by Master Alpin of Strathearn. This role had not previously existed in Scotland. Finally, Balliol's inauguration as King in November 1292 was performed by two of Edward's men, Anthony Bek and John de St John. This can be viewed as a case of Edward exerting his influence over Balliol and taken as evidence of Edward's involvement in Scottish affairs. This presented a significant challenge to Balliol as he began his reign as King of Scots.

It was clear that Edward planned on interfering in legal matters in Scotland. He humiliated Balliol by insisting that he would hear any complaints against Balliol's court. Unsurprisingly, there were a number of dissatisfied claimants from Scottish courts wishing to have unfavourable verdicts from Balliol, such as those on land grants, overturned by Edward.

The first legal case, in 1292, was from a **burgess** from Berwick. The burgess appealed three legal decisions made by the Guardians before Balliol became King. The burgess took his claim to Edward I who ruled in his favour and reversed one of the original decisions made by the Guardians. This was a serious embarrassment for Balliol because when government officials, such as the Earl of Buchan, Bishop Fraser, Patrick de Graham and Thomas Randolph, complained on behalf of Balliol when the appeal was made, their efforts backfired. They tried to use the terms of the agreement of Birgham to insist that Edward was overstepping his powers, as they asserted Scotland was an independent kingdom. Edward publicly forced Balliol to back down and issue letters proclaiming that the King of England was no longer bound to Birgham, or indeed any guarantees of Scottish independence. This essentially confirmed Edward's overlordship of Scotland and renounced any claims of Scottish independence.

However, the most embarrassing case was the McDuff case in 1293 when the younger son of Malcolm, Earl of Fife, claimed he had been denied possession of his lands and illegally imprisoned by Balliol. In a highly unusual move, Edward I forced Balliol to appear in person before him at Westminster and to answer the complaint from one of his own subjects. Edward would not allow Balliol the usual courtesy of having a representative to speak on his behalf. This was deeply undermining for Balliol as he was not being treated like a King, rather more like one of Edward's subjects. The case dragged on for two years as Balliol tried to refuse to testify personally. However, it was ended when Edward threatened to remove some of Balliol's castles in England. By this time, the Scottish court had been deeply humiliated. While it would not have been unusual for the King to have to testify in court if the case had been about the lands he kept in England (although some respect of rank would have been expected), it was highly unusual to be forced to answer a case from one of Balliol's own subjects outside of his kingdom, and it demonstrated the power Edward was intent on holding over Balliol's ability to distribute law and order in Scotland.

Edward I forced Balliol to pay him homage three times, undermining his rule by granting Edward political, economic and military overlordship in Scotland. First, Balliol was forced to acknowledge Edward as his overlord at Norham before he would be considered in the selection of the new King of Scots. Second, Balliol had to reaffirm his oath straight after his inauguration at Edward's parliament in Newcastle in 1292. This was a significant blow early on in his reign as no doubt Balliol, like all claimants to the Scottish throne, had hoped that the submission to Edward at Norham would be temporary, and certainly Edward had strongly hinted this at the time. However, the formal ceremony, across the border in England, suggested no such thing. Finally, it was in May 1295 at the Michaelmas parliament at Westminster that Balliol, although defiant and refusing the summons at first for the McDuff trial, renewed his homage to Edward. This was following a stern warning and insults from the English King that Balliol could lose three major castles and **burghs** if he refused to follow Edward's orders. This demonstrates the practical way in which Edward was exercising overlordship over Balliol and the kingdom of Scotland, undermining Balliol and his rule.

2.3 The Scottish response

Several powerful families in Scotland were dissatisfied with the level of power that Edward I was able to influence over Scotland. Robert Bruce VII, the future King, his father and his grandfather (Robert the Competitor who had put forward his claim for kingship in the Great Cause) were trying to strike a balance between holding their land and power in Scotland and satisfying a dominant Edward I of England. As well as their lands in Carrick and the south-west of Scotland, the Bruces held land in England. This was common for most lords in Scotland, including the Comyns, and was not seen as a problem. However, this situation would change in the build-up of tension between Balliol and Edward. Indeed, when Balliol rejected his fealty to Edward I and war broke out, lords were forced to choose between sole allegiance to the Scottish or the English King.

Balliol and his Comyn advisers looked to strengthen and centralise Scottish government to prevent appeals going to Edward I. At Balliol's second parliament (August 1293), his administration made a general call to all Scottish subjects to let them know that he would remedy any wrongs of justice directly, so there was no need to turn to Edward. This may well have been Balliol over-promising. Balliol also summoned all tenants-in-chief who had acquired lands after the death of Alexander III to come to the parliament to claim and evidence their rights to the land they owned. These lands were then placed in the hands of the local sheriff until the next parliament, held in Edinburgh in May 1294, in order to validate their claims. Although this was a long process, it suggests that the Balliol–Comyn administration was trying to strengthen Balliol's domestic legal position within Scotland. By the end of 1294, it could be argued that Balliol had managed to secure his administration and preserve peace in Scotland.

It is claimed in English chronicles that, late in 1294, Pope Celestine V granted Scottish lords an absolution from their oaths of homage to Edward I. Scotland was to become the Pope's 'special daughter' and its Church was to be free of English involvement. It is worth noting that the words of this document have been lost, but some historians believe that this **papal** decision reaffirmed the position of Scotland that had been established in 1192. This meant that in future dealings with England, the Scots would have protection from the papacy.

2.4 The Anglo-French War and the Franco-Scottish Treaty

Edward I's proposed war with France in 1294 led to open conflict between Scotland and England; John Balliol was caught between Scottish nobles who refused to fight for another King and his own loyalty as Edward's subject.

Edward I and the French King Philip IV went to war over Philip's decision to confiscate Edward's lucrative French **duchy** of Aquitaine. In June 1294, Edward sent a letter of summons for Balliol, as well as 10 Scottish earls and 16 barons, to assemble at Portsmouth on 1 September 1294 and be ready to fight for the English King against the French 'with horses and arms'. This was a significant turning point in the relationship between Balliol and Edward. No Scottish King had ever been compelled to fight under an English flag. However, as a landholder in England, and through his oaths of homage, it was clear Balliol could owe military service to Edward. The real distinction is that Balliol was being called up not simply as an English landowner holding his land directly from the King of England, but as King of Scots with the expectation that he would lead a Scottish force. Edward's demand for military service from the King of Scots was radically new.

English chroniclers state that Balliol originally agreed to Edward I's request for military aid; however, when Balliol approached his nobility with the idea, it became clear the Scots would not fight for Edward. Scotland had a lucrative wool trade and historical family links to Flanders in France. To go to war with France would cut off this trade and end good relations with the country. Fundamentally though, to fight for another King, in a war that was nothing to do with Scotland, was too much of a humiliation for the Scottish nobility.

Balliol held lands in England and in France, each with an estimated value of roughly £1,000 per year. To go to war with one country would certainly mean losing land and power in the other. Although Balliol had spent even more time in his French estate than in Scotland, his English land in Northumberland and Durham had been the home of his family for generations and so, it seemed, he would look to retain his lands there. Either way, he was going to have to choose a side.

In July 1295 the Scots called a parliament to discuss Edward I's request for military aid. Although still a highly debated topic, it is thought that around this time Balliol was sidelined from power and a council of 12 lords was appointed to help navigate the crisis. We can only speculate at the make-up of this council; however, it is known that Bishop Fraser, Matthew, Bishop of Dunkeld, Sir John de Soules and Sir Enguerrand de Umfraville (who were all on good terms with Balliol) were 'appointed' by Balliol to go to King Philip of France to organise an alliance.

The alliance with France was sealed on 23 February 1296 and ratified at Dunfermline by Balliol, the Comyn faction of nobles and many burgesses and bishops. To secure the alliance, Balliol's son and heir, Edward Balliol, was betrothed to King Philip of France's niece, Jeanne Valois, and Balliol was offered in the region of £6,000. By sealing this treaty, later viewed by some as the beginning of the 'Auld Alliance', Balliol was severing himself from Edward's service permanently, although at this stage it is unclear if he had any other choice.

Although the Auld Alliance is heralded as the start of Scotland's collective resistance to English overlordship, the treaty did not treat both parties equally. If Edward I found out about the treaty, it was most likely because Philip revealed it to him in the hope that Edward would remove some of his troops from France and send them to Scotland. However, whether he knew about it or not, Edward was unable to react with force immediately as he had to put down a major rebellion in Wales, led by Madog ap Llywelyn. However, he sent proxies to the Edinburgh parliament to demand troops. Once the Welsh rebellion was over, Edward once again set his sights north of the border.

2.5 The subjugation of Scotland, 1296

During the winter of 1295–96, nobles in Scotland and England prepared for war. Many noblemen had land in Scotland and England. With this came the knowledge that Edward I's government was more intrusive than John Balliol's government. In other words, in Scotland, the nobility had much more local power and freedom. The last thing many of them would have wanted was to see Edward take control of Scotland. The Comyns also supported Balliol because they had close family ties. Although the Bruce family and their allies supported King Edward, this was because of their rivalry with the Balliols and the Comyns. Overwhelmingly, the Scottish nobility did not want Edward I to govern Scotland.

In March 1296, those loyal to Balliol invaded the north of England and attacked Carlisle, which was defended by Robert Bruce VII (who had been installed as the governor of Carlisle Castle) on behalf of King Edward I. Balliol's forces laid **siege** to the castle, but Bruce's forces withstood the attack and, without the resources to continue, Balliol's forces had to retreat to Scotland. In response, Edward led his army to Berwick.

Berwick, the wealthiest burgh in Scotland, was prepared for conflict by reinforcing its already strong defences. Balliol and his supporters rushed more troops in from Lothian and Fife, assembling 10,000 men altogether. Their army was confident;

however, they had little experience in large-scale siege warfare of this kind. Edward I reached the border town of Coldstream on 28 March 1296. When he reached the town of Berwick, he offered the townspeople three days to consider surrender. The inhabitants responded by shouting insults at Edward, which led him to attack. The defenders were quickly overrun and it appears that there were few survivors because Berwick had to be repopulated with English tradesmen and merchants from Northumbria. This was the first key way that Edward subdued Scotland. Berwick was one of the most important trading ports and a major point of defence for the Scottish realm. Edward's attack was brutal, and he ordered no one to be spared. It is suggested that over 15,000 townspeople were killed. This was a major first victory for Edward I; it gave him control of a major port and demonstrated how brutal his campaign would be.

Edward I then went on to take control of the rest of Scotland. The next major castle was Dunbar in April 1296. The Earl of Dunbar had agreed to support Edward and promised to give him the keys to Dunbar Castle. However, the Earl's wife (a Comyn) supported the Scottish cause and she returned the keys to the castle warden in his absence before Edward's troops arrived. Edward's **vanguard**, led by the Earl of Surrey, William de Warenne, found a sizeable defensive army at the castle. The vanguard left some soldiers to keep watch and moved the rest of Edward's troops to a more favourable position to prepare to fight. Balliol's army mistook the opposing army's movement into battle formation for a retreat, so broke ranks and rushed towards Edward's army – giving up their advantageous position on higher ground. Edward's better trained and prepared army easily defeated Balliol's forces. Many of the Guardians and over 130 Scottish nobles were taken prisoner. This was another huge success for Edward as the loss of these leaders of the Scottish resistance to Edward's invasion meant support and enthusiasm for the war declined. Other commanders lost heart and surrendered. Balliol was unable to provide effective central leadership for them.

SOURCE 1

The Battle of Dunbar was fought on 27 April, where Patrick Graham and many nobles fell wounded. And a great many other knights and barons fled to Dunbar Castle in the hope of saving their lives, and were readily given shelter there. All in all there were 70 knights, as well as famous armed men, together with William Earl of Ross. The warden of that castle, however, Richard Siward by name, handed them over to the King of England like sheep offered for slaughter.

From a history of the Scottish kingdom written in Latin sometime between 1363 and c.1380 (probably in the mid-1360s). Although this work is lost, it was copied by the authors of texts that survive, which makes it possible in some places to reconstruct what it said. This translation was made by Dauvit Broun for this book.

Following Dunbar, Edward I's army marched along the east coast of Scotland, taking the key castles of Roxburgh, Edinburgh and Stirling in quick succession. By the end of July 1296, Edward had reached Elgin. Balliol had travelled to the north-east following his defeat at Dunbar in order to stay safe in Comyn lands. However, as he could not protect the castles, he told the Scots to do whatever they needed to protect themselves. So they did not offer much by way of resistance, contributing to the success of Edward's campaign.

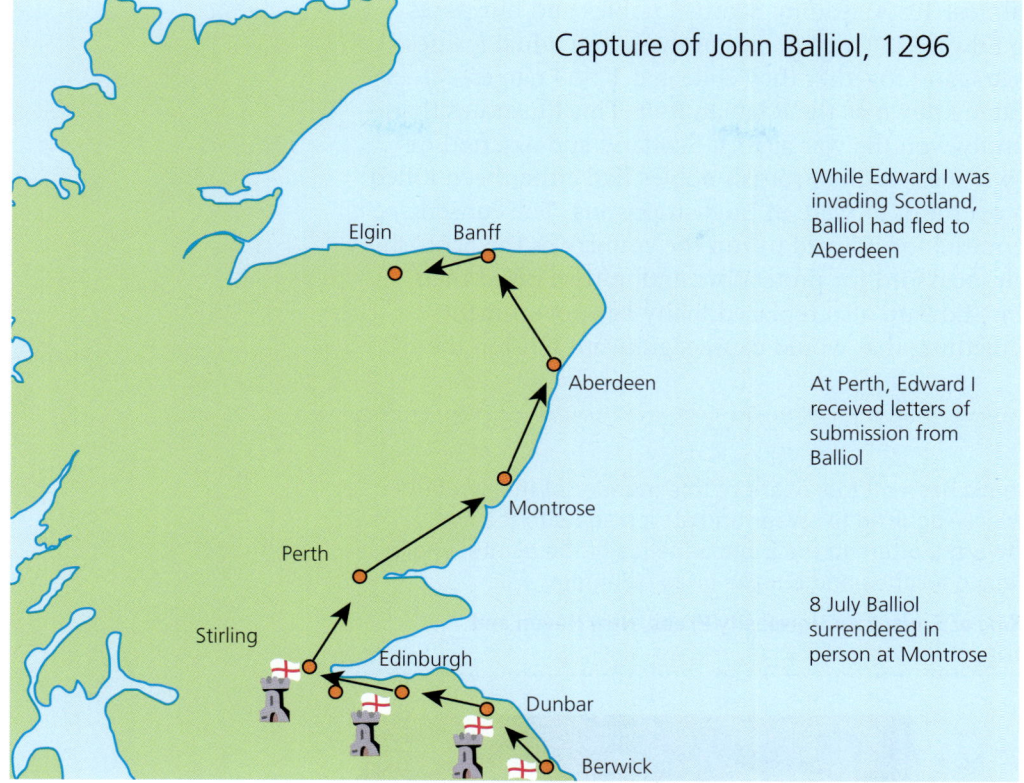

Figure 2.2 This map shows the route that Edward I travelled in 1296 during his conquest of Scotland.

On 2 July, Balliol offered his surrender in a letter sent to Edward I. At Forfar Castle, John Comyn met Edward and asked for his peace and protection. It was John Comyn who brought John Balliol and his son, Edward Balliol, from Aberdeen to Montrose Castle. On 10 July 1296, at Brechin Castle, Balliol was forced to surrender publicly in a humiliating ceremony. He apologised to Edward and gave up his throne and the kingdom of Scotland. Edward symbolically removed all of the symbols and badges, including the Seal of Scotland, which showed Balliol was King, giving him the nickname 'Toom Tabard' or 'Empty Coat'. This was the ultimate humiliation for Balliol and effectively marked the end of his personal rule.

Balliol, along with his son and heir, Edward Balliol, was imprisoned in the Tower of London, before being **exiled** to France in July 1299.

Edward I quickly took away any indication that Scotland was an independent country by removing the symbols of Scotland's independence. First, the Stone of Destiny, on which Scottish Kings were inaugurated, was taken to Westminster. This was a symbolic removal of the Scots' ability to enthrone their own King. Second, other important items of independent Scottish kingship were also taken to England, including Scotland's most treasured relic, the Holy Rood of St Margaret. This removed the very symbols of Scotland's independent identity. Medieval Scotland was deeply religious, and relics and ceremony were important parts of both the monarch's and everyday Scots' lives. The removal of these items was a clear signal to everyone in Scotland that Edward I was now in charge.

Finally, in late August 1296, almost 1,600 leading Scottish nobles and burgesses swore a personal oath to King Edward I. Three copies of these individual fealties were made in the following years, and together they collected 1,600 names. Collectively, these fealties became known as the Ragman Roll. This illustrates that, by 1296, Edward had successfully won the war against Scotland and asserted his power over the country. This was clear as the Scottish nobles had either been killed or forced to accept Edward as overlord, or were in English prisons. The consent of the Scottish nobility was required for Edward to run the country as the Scottish common people relied on their local lord for protection, and in turn owed their loyalty to their lord. Saying this, Edward also replaced many key government officials with his own men, something that would cause significant tension the following year.

> ### SOURCE 2
>
> Defeated, Scots in 1296 may have been all too aware of this plunder of the symbols of Scottish kingship, as they were required to swear and attach seals to their recorded oaths of fealty to Edward I, often on the Bible or relics of the saints, and at gatherings in important castles, churches and burghs or royal lands.
>
> M. Penman, *Robert the Bruce, King of Scots*, Yale University Press, New Haven and London, 2014.

Figure 2.3 The items above are seals from the nobility of Scotland. They were used to authenticate documents such as treaties letters. They were also used to ensure that letters remained unopened before they got to their intended recipients. The nobles of Scotland would have been made to attach their seals to the Ragman Roll to demonstrate that they paid homage to Edward I.

Figure 2.4 The stone of Scone is a replica of the Stone of Destiny at Scone Palace. The original was taken to Westminster Abbey by Edward I. It currently resides in Edinburgh Castle but will be returned to Perth in 2024.

By the end of 1296, Edward I had fully taken control of Scotland. Whereas Scotland could be considered to have been a vassal kingdom since Balliol became King, it was now directly administered by Edward. Edward did not **annex** Scotland in the same way that he had annexed Wales in 1284. Here, he had reduced the principality of Wales to the north-west corner of Wales and appointed his heir, Edward II, as Prince of Wales. However, Edward did write to Pope Boniface VIII five years later, in 1301, stating that he was in possession of the kingdom of Scotland, and by 1305 it was referred to as a land, rather than a kingdom.

Michael Lynch sums up the end of this period by saying:

> ### SOURCE 3
>
> The precise constitutional position remained in doubt for some time after 1296 ... However, there was little doubt of the practical consequences of English victory. King John was literally stripped of his status ... The Great Seal was broken up and the contempt of the conqueror was tellingly revealed by Edward's own words 'A man does good business when he rids himself of a turd.'
>
> **Michael Lynch,** *Scotland: A New History*, **Pimlico, London, 1992.**

ACTIVITIES

1. **a** Identify three events in which Edward I undermined John Balliol's authority before he marched north to Scotland in 1296.
   b For each of these events, explain what effect it would have had on Balliol's control of Scotland.
   c Rank the events on the arrow below from the 'worst' event to the 'best' event in terms of the damage they caused to his regime.

2. Copy the image of the map below into your jotter. Label the map according to the following instructions:
   a Label the towns of Edinburgh, Perth, Dunbar, Roxburgh, Stirling, Brechin and Elgin.
   b Draw an arrow to show Edward I's march through Scotland during the subjugation of 1296.
   c Draw a symbol at Berwick and Dunbar to remind yourself there was a battle there.

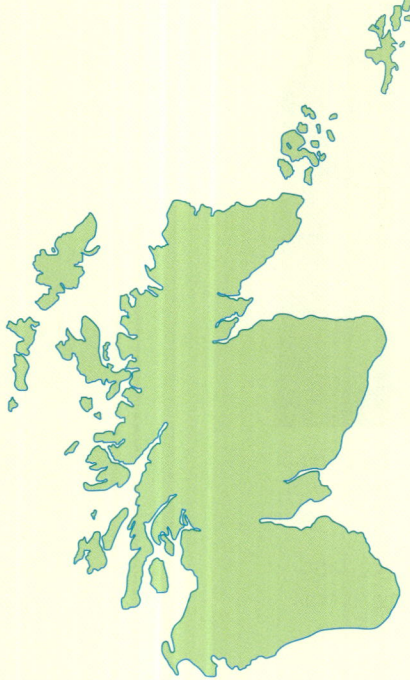

3. Copy the graph below and complete it using the information in this chapter. The X axis is time Balliol was in power and the Y axis is how much power he had in that year. Plot the main events from the chapter on the graph.

4. Answer the questions below in full sentences.
   a What was the height of John Balliol's power as King? Explain why this was in three sentences.
   b When was his power at its lowest? Draw an image to represent your answer.
   c How would you describe the journey of Balliol's political career in three sentences? Three words? One word?

GLOSSARY

Term	Meaning
annex	To add (territory) to one's own territory.
burgess	A merchant who is a member of the elite who control a burgh and who has special trading privileges (e.g. exemption from levies on trade).
burgh	A town with its own local government and laws, and rights to control trade in its locality.
duchy	An area of land – people who own duchies are normally dukes or duchesses.
enthrone	To formally place in a position of power – Scottish Kings were enthroned, they were not crowned.
exile	To remove or expel someone from their native country, normally as a punishment.
kin	People joined in mutual support as they are family.
papal	Something relating to the Pope in Rome.
siege	A military operation in which enemy forces surround a town or castle, cutting off essential supplies, with the aim of compelling those inside to surrender.
vanguard	The front group of soldiers of an advancing army.

Chapter 3

William Wallace and the Scottish resistance

The aim of this chapter is to consider the role of William Wallace and the Scottish resistance to the overlordship of Edward I between 1297 and 1305.

LINK TO EXAM

Higher

Key issue 3: William Wallace and the Scottish resistance

Background

The subjugation of Scotland in 1296 resulted in John Balliol, King of Scots, being ceremonially stripped of his power and authority as King. Edward I asserted his right as overlord of Scotland to take Scotland into his possession and rule it directly. After the siege of Berwick and the Battle of Dunbar, Scottish resistance crumbled in the face of the power of Edward. The castles of Roxburgh, Edinburgh and Stirling fell quickly and, by July 1296, King John I and his closest advisers had surrendered at Montrose and had been imprisoned in the Tower of London. Edward took over direct government of Scotland, in effect abolishing the Scottish kingdom. Though he would lose control of most of Scotland in 1297, he successfully re-conquered the kingdom and created a more long-term government in 1305.

Edward I conquered Scotland in 1296 and, after 1,600 Scottish landholders swore loyalty to him for their lands, he began to rule Scotland directly through a government of occupation. The symbolically important Stone of Destiny was taken to Westminster, alongside other insignia of Scottish independence. Edward had subdued Scotland in a matter of months, between April and August of 1296, and made the majority of Scottish lords pledge homage to him. Soon 131 Scottish nobles, including King John Balliol and the Earls of Ross and Atholl and Menteith, were in English prison. The Comyns, the most powerful family in the Scottish government, had been sent to take 'hunting leave' on their estates in England. Edward I's officials were despatched to Scotland to run its affairs: Hugh Cressingham acted as treasurer, the Earl of Surrey as royal lieutenant, and the chancellor, Walter Amersham, together governed Scotland. Edward's power seemed absolute. Edward's allies controlled the law, castles and the most important land in the kingdom of Scotland.

However, the geopolitical reality was somewhat different. Edward I was fighting a war on two fronts, both in Scotland and in France. This had been hugely expensive for Edward's kingdom and, more importantly, by 1297 the war in France was going badly. Protests at home were mounting from Edward's nobles with some earls refusing to send troops as Edward charged more and more tax to fund the war. The general tax he tried to impose had no backing in parliament, and the fierce backlash against his actions reaffirmed the need for parliament to approve taxes of this nature. This was part of the context in which a number of uprisings and disturbances broke out in Scotland in 1297.

William Wallace and the Scottish resistance

For the exam, it is important to understand the attempts William Wallace and the Scottish resistance made to resist English rule before 1305. This chapter will examine the early Scottish resistance in the north, south, east and west to the rule of Edward I. It will then go on to examine the roles of Wallace and Andrew Moray in the Scottish resistance. Wallace and Moray were responsible for the victory at Stirling Bridge against Edward's army. Its effects on Scots and on Scotland will be examined. This victory was followed by defeat at Falkirk and continuing resistance until the death of Wallace in 1305, which will also be explored here.

The discussion in this chapter will be divided into the following areas of interest:
- 3.1 Scottish resistance
- 3.2 Roles of William Wallace and Andrew Moray
- 3.3 Victory at Stirling Bridge and its effect on Scots and on Scotland
- 3.4 Defeat at Falkirk and continuing Scottish resistance

3.1 Scottish resistance

Throughout the spring and summer of 1297 there was significant resistance to Edward I's rule in Scotland from a variety of groups in Scottish society. By 1297, the Earl of Surrey had been forced to bring a substantial army north of the border to quell the threat of the uprisings. During this period, Edward was fighting a war against France and was not in England. Some historians argue that his lack of attention to Scotland allowed the early resistance to flourish. This section will examine the cause of the resistance, the various uprisings and the impacts of the resistance on Scotland.

By May of 1297, it was clear Edward I's rule in Scotland was beginning to crumble. The Earl of Surrey was not interested in governing Scotland. He did not leave his Yorkshire estates for he hated the weather in Scotland and complained that it was bad for his health. The real power lay with Hugh Cressingham. Within nine months of Cressingham's appointment, he had sent £5,188, a huge sum, to England, money which he had collected from Scottish tax. Historically, the Scots had not been taxed heavily and so this unprecedented sum caused tension with the Scottish nobility and smaller landowners who felt Cressingham had no right to demand it.

From April 1297, Edward I's regime also began to seize wool (with the promise to pay later) to be sold at profit to fund the war with France. As wool was Scotland's main source of economic wealth, this caused widespread anger throughout the kingdom. By 1297, Cressingham was complaining that Scots were refusing to pay any tax at all, leaving their English officials in debt and unable to pay their own troops.

Furthermore, 57 Scottish nobles were summoned to serve in Flanders on 24 May, and it was declared that any Scot still imprisoned in England after Dunbar could serve with Edward I in return for his freedom. This, in addition to rumours that Edward was planning to send Scottish troops from the '**middling folk**' of society to France to fight for him, galvanised the Scottish resistance to Edward's regime.

Some of the first displays of resistance to Edward I's regime happened in the north-west of Scotland, throughout Argyll and the Western Isles. In Argyll, the regional rivalry between ruling families led to unrest. Under the reign of Alexander III, the MacDougalls of Argyll had traditionally been the strongest family in the Argyll region. However, this clan and the MacRuaridhs of Garmoran reacted violently to the installation of the MacDonalds as Edward's agents in the area. Alexander MacDonald and Angus Og had become Edward's chief agents in the region since the fall of the Balliol regime. This left the MacDougalls expelled from patronage but not powerless. On their release from imprisonment in May 1297, Alexander MacDougall and his son John launched a vicious attack on the MacDonald territories in retaliation. By the summer of 1297, the MacDonalds were struggling to restrain the widespread MacDougall rebellion, and the violence threatened to spill into Clydeside. These powerful families in the west would initially support the removal of the English forces from Scotland, putting pressure on Edward's control of the north of the country.

Robert Bruce VI, Earl of Carrick, had retired to his estates in England. His son Robert Bruce VII, the new Earl of Carrick and future King of Scots, expected some repayment for his family's support of Edward I's campaign in Scotland. However, this never materialised. In June 1297, Robert Bruce VII was sent to make another oath of loyalty to Edward at Carlisle. Oaths were sworn before God as Scotland was a highly religious society. Bruce was therefore allowed to return to his lands in Annandale as Edward did not expect him to break such a sacred vow. Here, to make it look like he was carrying out Edward's government, he rode to the land of a supporter of resistance, William Douglas. Bruce VII set Douglas's estate on fire and took his wife and children, including his eldest son, back to the Bruces' seat at Annandale. William Douglas was working with the Wallace rebellion further north (explored on page 38) and historians believe this was a move to keep Douglas's family safely away from Edward, rather than Bruce VII carrying out Edward's justice.

Once Robert Bruce VII returned, he began his rebellion by breaking his oath to Edward I and making a passionate appeal to his father's men to fight against him. However, these men's loyalties were to Bruce's father, and most refused to support the young Bruce. Despite this lack of support, Bruce VII travelled north and raised an army in his own lands of Carrick. James Stewart joined him, as did another former Guardian of Scotland, Bishop Robert Wishart of Glasgow, who was determined to maintain Scottish independence. Together they began to attack English garrisons in the south-west. This was a problem for Edward as Bruce, Stewart and Wishart were important Scottish **magnates** whom he wanted to keep under control to prevent further organised rebellion.

However, by midsummer 1297, Edward I's forces led by Henry Percy and Robert Clifford had managed to subdue the rebellion and force Robert Bruce VII, Wishart, Douglas and Stewart to broker a peace arrangement at Irvine on the Ayrshire coast. The peace arrangement was proposed on 7 July and stated that Bruce was to hand over his daughter Marjorie as a hostage to ensure his further support of Edward. Wishart and Stewart were to be guarantors in case Bruce failed to fulfil the peace arrangement. The men did not dispute Edward's right to rule Scotland but complained about his treatment of the country, including his demands for military service and ignorance of its laws and customs. Bruce never gave his daughter as hostage, instead drawing out negotiations over the arrangement. Walter of Guisborourgh, a chronicler writing a few years later, suggests that the drawn-out discussions were stalling tactics to allow William Wallace time to withdraw from Selkirk with his troops. It is likely, then, that Bruce was still actively aiding the Wallace and Moray rebellion during the rest of 1297. Negotiations lasted almost a month, allowing Wallace to gather more men. Although Wishart and Douglas were taken into captivity, Bruce and Stewart were allowed to return to their lands.

One big reason for the success of the early resistance to Edward I's rule was the lack of organisation among his officials placed in charge of Scotland. Hugh Cressingham had raised an army of 300 cavalry and 10,000 foot soldiers to subdue the noble revolt in the west. However, when he arrived at the muster point of Roxburgh he was met by Percy and Clifford who were convinced they had negotiated victory at Irvine and restored order in Scotland. They convinced Cressingham that his force was not required and that they should wait until the Earl of Surrey came up from the south. As the three men were of roughly equal rank, it was agreed they would wait for Surrey before further action was taken against the rebelling Scots. This delay enabled the resistance to Edward's rule to continue.

3.2 Roles of William Wallace and Andrew Moray

William Wallace and Andrew Moray are the two most notable figures of this period. They led the Scottish resistance to Edward I in 1297. Both of these men were inspirational and charismatic people in their own right and inspired many Scots to fight against Edward's government of occupation. Importantly, they both were fighting for the restoration of Balliol to his rightful place as King and held no desire to become King in their own right.

It is said that William Wallace 'raised his head' in April of 1297. This is an appropriate image for a man who does not have a well-documented background. Most of what we know about Wallace is from a fifteenth-century poem called 'The Wallace', written by a poet known as Blind Harry. The old Blind Harry tradition that Wallace was from Elderside has been proven false. Although little is known of Wallace, analysis of his seal in the 1990s revealed that his father was called Alan and was a landholder from Ayrshire. This means that Wallace's father was not a knight, but, if it is Alan Wallace, then his name can be found on the Ragman Roll, which supports the idea that he must have had some standing as a landholder. The emblem on Wallace's seal, which was a bow and arrow, indicates he was a skilled archer, hunter or perhaps a solider. While there is no evidence to suggest Wallace was an 'outlaw', as described by English chroniclers, there is some evidence that he sometimes lived outside the law. For example, he is mentioned in English records as a 'thief' active near Perth a week before Edward I arrived there in June 1296.

Figure 3.1 This is a representation of Wallace (c. 1272–76 to 1305) from *The National and Domestic History of England* by William Aubrey, published London c. 1890. Wallace defeated Edward I at Stirling Bridge but was himself defeated at Falkirk in 1298. Although we have descriptions of Wallace, we do not know exactly what he looked like and so rely on artists' interpretations to give us some idea.

What is sure is that Wallace was fighting for the restoration of King John Balliol when he began his rebellion. This was important as it made Wallace's rebellion legitimate in the eyes of the Scottish nobility and so they supported his endeavours.

The first recorded resistance was on 3 May 1297. Wallace and his co-leader, the noble Sir Richard of Lundie, accompanied by 30 other men, killed Edward I's official in the area, William Heselrig, the sheriff of Lanark. According to Andrew Wyntoun, who wrote his account nearly a century later, Heselrig's murder was triggered because the sheriff killed Wallace's wife, although there is some speculation this might be romanticised. The murder of Heselrig was considered **treason**, as an assault on an English official was considered akin to an assault on Edward himself.

Wallace then went over 80 miles north where he joined with William Douglas and together they attacked English-controlled Scone. Douglas was a nobleman who was the commander of the Scottish garrison at Berwick in 1296. Here, they attempted to kill a more important official, William Ormsby, who was Edward I's chief judge in Scotland. Although Ormsby escaped, they managed to capture valuables and horses before making for Selkirk Forest which provided a nearly impenetrable cover. It is clear that Percy and Clifford underestimated Wallace, who was left to build his army at Selkirk. The position of the English forces in the north-east became so perilous that the English sheriff, Henry de Latham, decided to join the Scottish resistance.

Other revolts in the north-east, particularly in the region of Moray around Inverness, were important in the early resistance to Edward I. These were led by Sir Andrew Moray, who was a charismatic young leader and a member of the **aristocracy**. Moray was trained as a knight. He fought at Dunbar in 1296 and was captured alongside his father and put in prison in Chester. However, he somehow managed to escape and made his way back to his family lands near Inverness, rejoining the struggle against Edward I's regime. Andrew Moray was a supporter of Balliol and a member of the higher nobility in Scotland. His father, also Andrew, held one of the most important crown offices: the Justiciar of Scotia (Scotland north of the Forth). His uncle, William Moray, was the Lord of Bothwell. Other members of his family included prominent Church members. This greatly helped the campaign because it meant that others in the aristocracy supported him. His charismatic leadership style also gained him supporters from other sections of society.

> ### SOURCE 1
> We write to tell you how an insurrection has recently come about in Moray and other neighbouring lands under Andrew, son of Sir Andrew Moray, and others. We are letting you know that we are determined to promote peace and to put down the insurrection, and maintain these areas. And we consider yours and our own forces to be adequate for this task ... When we arrived at the town of Inverness, we sent a message to the Countess of Ross asking her to come and provide us with her own advice, power, and assistance for keeping the peace, in order to set royal justice in order so that she might gain your favour and thanks in the future. She readily agreed to our request and placed herself in our charge. And since she was faithful and friendly, we bear true witness to her good standing and her efforts and devotion towards you.
>
> **A letter to Edward I, sent from Inverness on 24 July 1297 from his men in the north-east of Scotland to tell him about a rebellion which was happening around Moray, led by Sir Andrew Moray. It also tells the King that the Countess of Ross, the wife of the Earl of Ross, a powerful noblewoman, has been very helpful in their efforts to stop the rebellion.**

Moray **raised his standard** against Edward I in Avoch, in the Black Isle, and led a **guerrilla** campaign capturing Urquhart Castle, Inverness, Elgin, Duffus and Banff. He had support from the Comyns of Badenoch, Lochaber and Buchan, the Earl of Mar, John, Earl of Atholl, as well as other burgesses and tenants loyal to his father, to fight against the English forces in the name of King John Balliol. By the summer of 1297, the resistance had successfully cleared out Edward I's administration in the north-east and retaken Aberdeen. Aberdeen was a major trading town and so this was a significant blow to Edward's control of Scotland. Moray's part in the Scottish Wars is sometimes overlooked because he died of his wounds two months after the Battle of Stirling Bridge. However, without this early success, the resistance movement in Scotland would not have been nearly as powerful.

Edward I was still fighting a war on two fronts. So on 11 June, in an effort to quickly resolve the issue of Moray's campaign in the north, Sir John Comyn of Badenoch and his cousin, the Earl of Buchan, were allowed to leave England to go home to deal with the threat of Badenoch's nephew, Sir Andrew Moray. Both had been held hostage and made to swear loyalty to Edward and so it was thought, perhaps misguidedly, that they would remain on Edward's side and stop Moray's rebellion. These men knew the land Moray was operating in well, giving them more chance of capturing him. However, they were unable to catch him and told Edward that when they confronted Moray, he took his troops into boggy conditions inaccessible to cavalry. This seemed unlikely and English forces were right to think that in fact the Scottish noblemen were not serving the King of England at all. Soon, Buchan openly changed sides and supported Moray's rebellion. Badenoch did not openly support the rebellion, because his son was fighting with Edward in Flanders, but he did not actively support Edward either. This was a major step forwards in the Scottish resistance, and a great achievement for Moray. The Comyn family had been at the centre of government in Scotland for many years and would be looked upon to provide leadership in any future agitation against Edward's occupation.

These seemingly disjointed revolts, mobilised by different leaders, enjoyed widespread support from all classes of Scottish society. By August 1297, Moray had joined Wallace in Dundee and successfully laid siege to Dundee Castle, removing the English garrison. This was the final garrison Edward I had held in the north of Scotland. The land south of the Forth remained under Edward's control. Dundee was vital to Scotland's commercial and social interactions with Europe and the Scottish resistance would need this connection if they were to request aid from Europe to help secure independence. While many Scottish noblemen could not openly support the rebellion, they certainly sent men to Wallace to support his campaign.

3.3 Victory at Stirling Bridge and its effect on Scots and on Scotland

Edward I either could not, or would not, return from France to deal with the threat in Scotland. However, the Scottish resistance could not possibly be ignored. Instead, he ordered the Earl of Surrey to remain in Scotland to quell the resistance. His order arrived the day after the Battle of Stirling Bridge.

Stirling Castle was one of the most geopolitically important castles in Scotland. It was known as the 'key to the north' because whoever wanted to travel north in Scotland had to pass by the castle. It was the easiest and cheapest route. Armies could not march up the west coast, for example, as it was difficult terrain and provided no food for travelling soldiers.

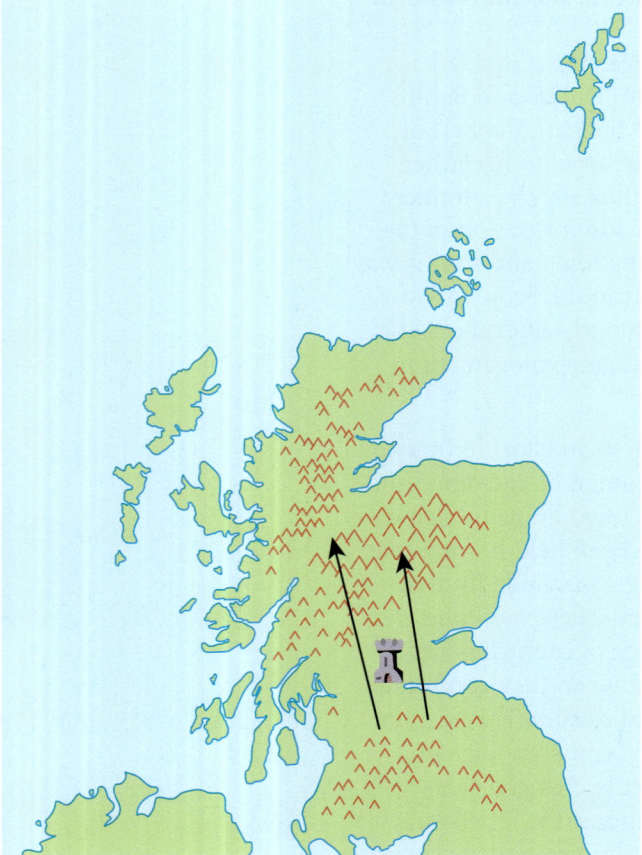

Figure 3.2 All routes north had to pass by Stirling Castle.

The west was also mountainous and had large rivers like the Clyde that were difficult to cross. The east was equally difficult to try to march through because the Firth of Forth cut deep inland, making the only way to cross by ferry, which was not practical for large armies. By the autumn of 1297, it was clear that if Edward I's army marched north to combat the Scottish resistance, it would march through Stirling.

Figure 3.3 Stirling Castle, in Stirling, today. The castle stands on a lump of volcanic rock and has a good vantage point. The castle was one of the most important in Scotland due to its geographical location.

Victory at Stirling

Edward I's army was made up of those men whom Cressingham had gathered in mid-July and those brought back to Berwick by Clifford and Percy from Irvine. Some Scottish nobles, including the Earl of Lennox and James Stewart, were also among Edward's numbers. Walter of Guisborough, a fourteenth-century chronicler, stated that the English army had far larger numbers than the Scots. However, recent historiography argues that these figures are likely overinflated. It is now generally agreed that the English army had 350 cavalry and 6,350 infantry, made up of knights, spear-men, longbow-men and archers. This made it smaller than the army raised for Dunbar, though it was still made up of professional soldiers. The English nobility were exhausted from war and getting more men even into France, let alone Scotland, was becoming impossible. The war in France was a far more exciting option than the war in cold and wet Scotland, so the majority of Edward's army were already abroad.

The Scottish army is estimated to have contained around 180 knights and light horsemen, and around 5,000 foot soldiers. Most of the Scottish horsemen would have been nobility who attended with Moray. The foot soldiers were comprised mainly of farmers. The laws of the Common Army of Scotland also meant that some would have been called to fight by their local noble landholder. There is evidence that some people were prepared to support Wallace against their lord's wishes, for example the men in Coldingham in Berwickshire. Robert Bruce VII was not at the battle: he was in hiding after he refused to give his daughter Marjorie across as a hostage, as agreed in the terms at Irvine. Overall though, this army was, in military terms, significantly weaker than the English army.

Cressingham and de Warenne, the Earl of Surrey, were Edward I's military commanders. Surrey had led the English forces to victory at Dunbar and was a skilled tactician. However, his health was declining and he utterly detested his position in cold and rainy Scotland. As the treasurer, it was no surprise that Cressingham did not have the military skill of his counterpart. The day before the battle, Cressingham sent some of the soldiers home to try to save on wages, as the cost of maintaining the forces in Scotland was already proving too expensive. It is fair to say that both commanders underestimated the Scottish force they were to confront.

On 11 September 1297, Stewart and Lennox tried to negotiate peace with the Scottish commanders; however, they were quickly turned away. Then two monks were sent to negotiate. They were told by Wallace to tell their leaders that 'we have not come for the sake of peace but are ready to fight for the vindication and freedom of our kingdom'.

Wallace and Moray had been styled the 'commanders of the army of the kingdom of Scotland' and both were considered inspirational and able leaders. Although Wallace is more famous than Moray today, there is no doubt that Moray's tactical skills were important in the outcome of the battle.

The English army was positioned on the south bank of the river, under the shadow of the castle which they still controlled. The Scottish army took position on the higher ground of the Abbey Craig. This offered an excellent vantage point to view the movements of the English army.

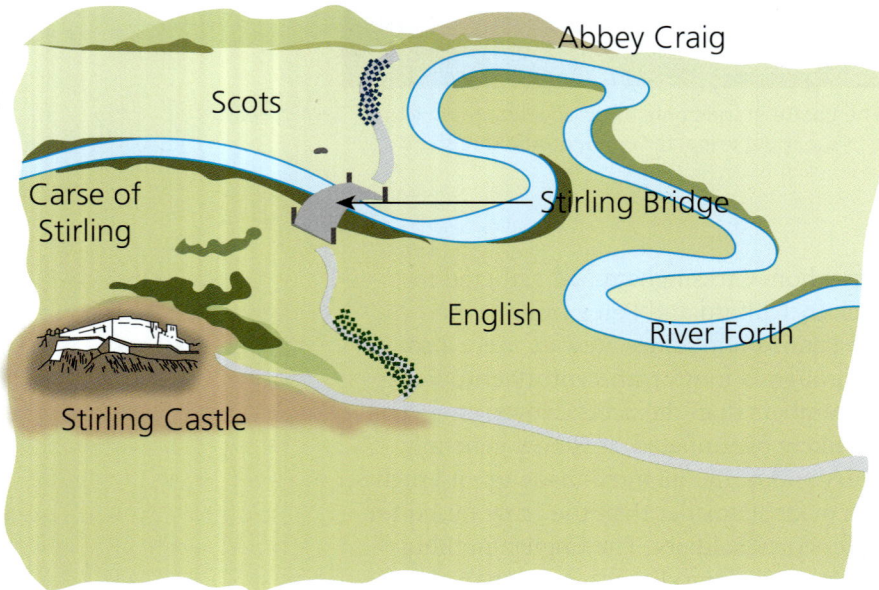

Figure 3.4 This image shows the starting positions of both armies at the Battle of Stirling. Notice the loop in the river that the English forces were marching into.

Surrey, presumably feeling unwell, slept in on the morning of the battle. Keen to subdue the Scots as quickly as possible to keep costs low, Cressingham had already ordered the soldiers to begin to cross the bridge by the time that Surrey woke up. They were hastily called back. Once Surrey arrived at the battlefront, he gave the order to cross the bridge for a second time. However, this was quickly cancelled in the hope that Lennox and Stewart, who had now arrived back in the English camp, had news of Wallace and Moray's capitulation. Wallace's message no doubt angered the English army leaders, and the army was now ordered to cross for what was a third time. However, Edward I's army had already given away their intention to cross the river to the Scottish troops watching on the hill above.

Richard Lundie, who had defected to Edward I's side after Irvine, tried to give the English commanders the benefit of his local knowledge. He, with others, opposed the plan to cross a third time and suggested a contingent of cavalry cross at a potentially safer ford upstream to outflank the Scottish forces. However, this was dismissed by both commanders. To save finances the commanders wanted to subdue the Scots as quickly as possible, and going upriver would mean further pay for the men and money spent on food. Second, any delay in outflanking the Scottish forces might have been viewed as nothing more than giving them a chance to slip away while Edward's army manoeuvred. It would also have been highly embarrassing if Edward's army were to march all the way to Stirling and not successfully engage the Scots in battle. Cressingham and Surrey did not want to be the cause of such an embarrassment. Chris Brown argues that 'Cressingham's decision to cross the river cannot be seen in any other light than an attempt to force battle on the enemy'.

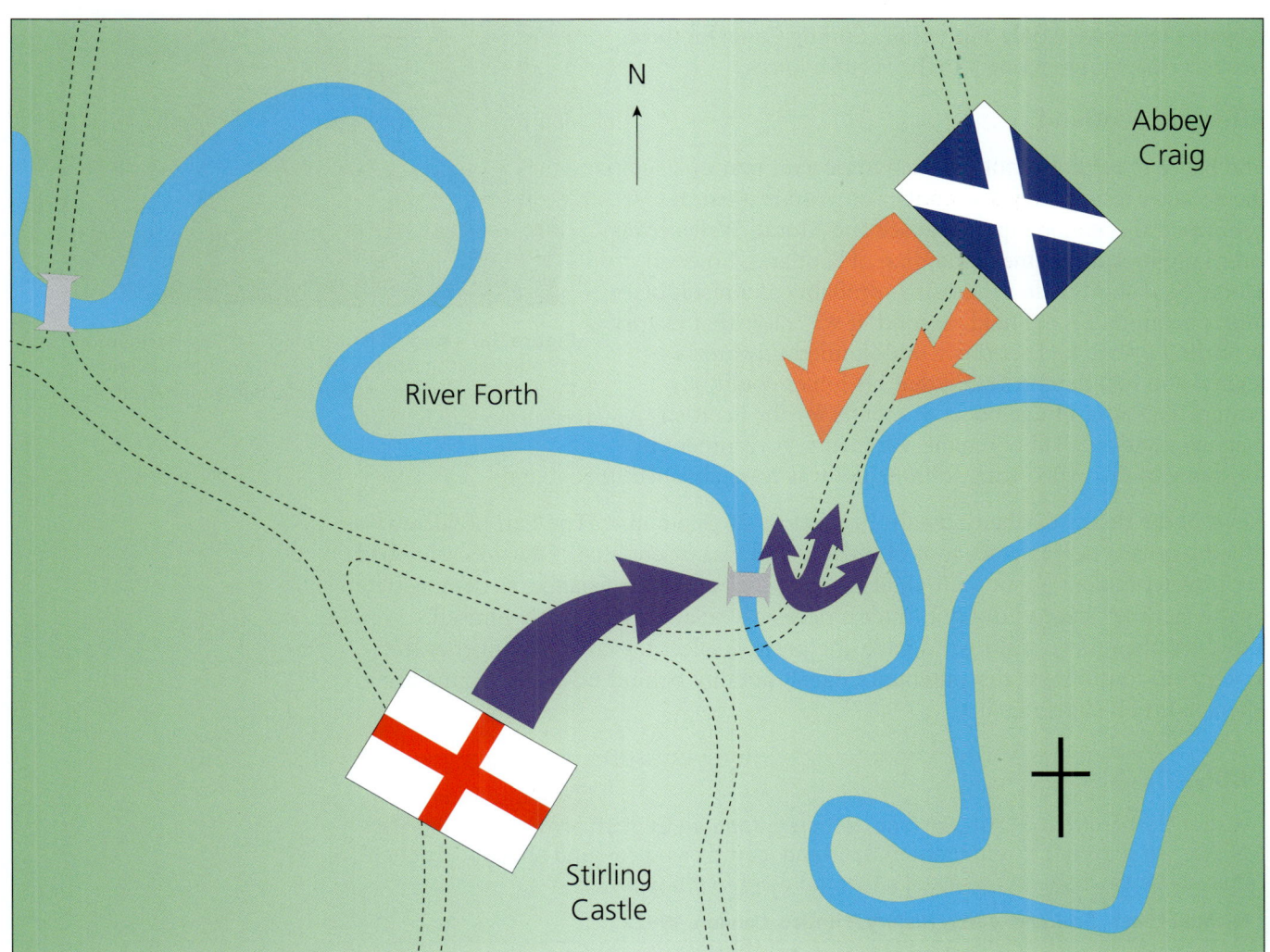

Figure 3.5 The movements of the English and Scottish forces at Stirling Bridge in 1297. Note how the English would be forced into the narrow loop of the river with nowhere to escape.

Surrey probably expected the Scottish resistance to wait until Edward I's army was over the bridge and lined up before commencing the battle. This was the traditional way of fighting. However, when roughly a third of the English troops had crossed, the Scottish forces attacked. The tactical situation suited the Scottish well and they were able to cut off the bottleneck of the river and force Edward's troops back into the boggy land. This part of the English forces was quickly cut off from the rest of the advancing army, and unable to retreat, they were either cut down or drowned in the river trying to escape. The casualties included Hugh de Cressingham himself. He was so hated in Scotland that he was **flayed** and his skin made into a sword sheath for Wallace's belt. The Scottish resistance had won and the remaining English army fled back to Berwick. Edward's forces were only able to hold Stirling Castle for three weeks, before surrendering it to the Scottish forces.

Effect on Scotland

The Battle of Stirling Bridge was an important part of the Scottish resistance for a number of reasons. First, it confirmed the leadership of Wallace and Moray. Wallace was later knighted and named Guardian of Scotland, however, Moray died shortly after the battle, probably as a result of an injury acquired on the field. Second, it was clear that victory at Stirling Bridge had seriously undermined Edward I's regime and had demonstrated that his forces could be beaten. This was a huge boost of morale for the Scottish magnates and the Balliol regime. After this, government in the name of the exiled King John Balliol was re-established in Scotland.

Figure 3.6 A map of Britain by Matthew Paris, monk and chronicler of St Albans (d. 1259). Scotland is joined to England by a bridge at Stirling, which demonstrates the importance of Stirling.

News of the defeat reached Edward I's court by 26 September. The Earl of Surrey was called to give a personal account of the loss and was discredited. Edward's army had been overconfident about their ability to beat the Scottish resistance, as demonstrated by the fact that Edward did not think it necessary to attend the battle himself. However, the loss at Stirling did have one positive effect for Edward. Anger at the loss served to unify the discontented English nobility behind Edward's regime again. Michael Lynch sums this up:

> ### SOURCE 2
> Wallace's victory at Stirling Bridge, inflicted upon an English army led by the Earl of Warren, Edward's lieutenant in Scotland, came as a profound shock to English opinion. In retrospect it marked a turning point in the wars.
>
> **Michael Lynch, *Scotland: A New History*, Pimlico, London, 1992.**

Writs were sent to the sheriff of York, 13 Scottish magnates including Comyn of Badenoch and the Earls of Dunbar, Angus, Strathearn, Menteith, Lennox, Buchan and Sutherland (although not to Carrick) to state that Sir Brian FitzAlan would lead them as a force against the 'rebel' Scots.

As Guardian, Wallace was not viewed as a replacement for the absent King John Balliol. Instead, he would be expected to make political decisions for the good of the realm. His first aim was to consolidate his position, so that he could carry out the other diplomatic, economic and legal duties he had acquired as Guardian.

Over the October and November of 1297, Wallace consolidated the Scottish position by attacking the north of England as far down as Stainmore against Clifford and the Bishop of Carlisle. This was not about controlling land. Rather, it was about feeding his army at the expense of the English people and embarrassing Edward I. Edward retaliated at Christmas of the same year. Clifford marched north with 7 knights, 16 **esquires** and 500 foot soldiers. They marched into Annandale, a region controlled by the Bruce family. At the same time, Bruce VI was sent to Scotland, probably with the aim of trying to convince his son to remain on the side of Edward I. Clifford left 100 foot soldiers north of the border to try to prevent a further Scottish attack. Aside from this, the Wallace administration was left alone in the months after Stirling as Edward had to attend to his own domestic issues.

Wallace also sought to solidify control domestically. The seat of Lothian continued to be controlled by Edward I's forces. Wallace marched his men into Lothian, and they were able to march through Haddington without stirring unrest or resistance from Edward's forces. On one hand, seeing a great Scottish army would give hope to those sympathetic to the Balliol cause and make the occupying regime look weak. On the other hand, the castles that fell to the Scottish army were all but handed over to Wallace without force. However, Edinburgh Castle, which stored royal treasures and archives, was far too strong to be captured without an extended siege and Wallace was not able to take it.

Wallace sought to establish normal peacetime functioning of a medieval government. While in Haddington, he and Moray wrote letters to merchants in the Baltic to encourage them to trade with Scotland again after the period of warfare. The surviving copy we have of one of these letters is called the Lubeck Letter, written to German merchants at Hamburg and Lübeck. In the letter Wallace and Moray style themselves as 'Andrew Moray and William Wallace, leaders of the army of the kingdom of Scotland, and the community of the same kingdom'. The letter demonstrates that Wallace was not only trying to boost trade and therefore the economy in Scotland, but also looking for international recognition of his rule.

Figure 3.7 The Lubeck Letter, with Wallace's seal as Guardian attached, 1297.

> **SOURCE 3**
>
> Haddington: 11 October 1297
>
> Andrew Moray and William Wallace, leaders of the army of the kingdom of Scotland and the community of the kingdom, to their friends the mayors and citizens of Lübeck and Hamburg: greeting.
>
> We have been told by trustworthy merchants of the kingdom of Scotland that you are giving advice, help and favour in all causes and business concerning us and our merchants, for which we thank you. We ask that you tell your merchants that they can have safe access to all the ports in the kingdom of Scotland, since Scotland (thanks be to God) has been rescued from the power of the English by force of arms.
>
> Farewell.
>
> **Transcript of the Lubeck Letter, 1297: Moray and Wallace write to merchants in Germany, thanking them for supporting Scottish merchants and telling them that safe trading can commence with Scotland as the country is no longer at war.**

Wallace also sought out potential allies in Europe. Wishart's man, William Lamberton, had been given the role of Bishop of St Andrews. He visited Rome and Paris in the name of Wallace and King John Balliol to try to convince the Pope to restore Balliol to his kingdom in Scotland.

3.4 Defeat at Falkirk and continuing Scottish resistance

Defeat at Falkirk

After dealing with his domestic issues, Edward I prepared to **muster** his army in Yorkshire at the end of May 1298. He set the scene for the invasion by inviting the Scottish magnates, who had sworn their oaths to him for homage, to come and fight for the English crown. Those who did not attend the muster at York had their lands forfeited, making Scotland an attractive proposition for those looking to acquire new land and titles. The Battle of Falkirk would mark the end of Wallace's time as Guardian. However, the Scottish resistance would continue.

Edward I had mustered an immense army of around 2,000 cavalry and around 12,000 foot soldiers for the Battle of Falkirk. This had been achieved because of the coming together of English nobles in the wake of Stirling Bridge, and because Edward had reissued Magna Carta, an acknowledgement that he had not treated them well. The army included well-trained foot soldiers, including Welsh longbowmen and archers. The English forces had three battle lines: a vanguard under Norfolk and Hereford, the rearward battle under the Bishop of Durham and the main battle under Edward. This was a significant fighting force by medieval standards.

Wallace's army was made up of many Stirling Bridge veterans. Wallace divided them into four circular **schiltrons** of around 1,500 men each. These were hedgehog-like formations with spearmen standing shoulder to shoulder, holding their spears facing outwards in a circle. The spears were deadly for mounted knights. Between these schiltrons were archers from Selkirk Forest led by John Stewart, James Stewart's brother. The Scottish cavalry, led by the Comyns, was at either side of the schiltrons. At their back was Callander Wood, which would be used to provide cover in the event of retreat.

The Battle of Falkirk took place on 22 July 1298. The start of the battle went well for Wallace. Edward I's massive army was underfed and needed provisions, more than it could carry, and it was usual for these to be bought – or taken – on conquest from the local area. However, Wallace employed the tactic of 'scorched earth', which involved the burning of fields, grass and hills and the removal of all animals from the land so it was barren when Edward's army descended upon it. Wallace planned on starving Edward's army into retreat. By July 1298, unfavourable winds meant that Edward's supply ships had not reached him in time. When they did arrive, a large part of the delivery was wine, which resulted in fighting between the Welsh and the English troops. All of this meant that Edward I's army was weakened by the time they reached Wallace.

Wallace was nearly successful in his aim. Edward I had decided to retreat to Edinburgh to get supplies for his troops and await news of Wallace. However, news came on 21 July that Edward's spies had found Wallace, camped at Kirkliston, only 10 miles from Edward's army. Wallace knew of Edward's plan to go to Edinburgh and planned to attack the English forces at night. However, Edward marched to the waiting Scots, meeting them near Falkirk. The Earls of Angus and Dunbar had been key in giving away Wallace's position, demonstrating that not all Scottish people were on Wallace's side.

Wallace understood that the mounted knights were the most dangerous of Edward I's retinue. He placed his army in a strong position on the hillside, with a bog in front to avoid a direct advance. The schiltrons seemed to be effective at first, holding a cavalry charge from Hereford's vanguard, which was forced to move to the westerly side of the Scottish army. The second line, headed by Durham, went around the bog to the easterly side and also attacked, losing many cavalry. At this moment, the Scottish cavalry fled the battlefield without making any contact with the English army. Certainly, these nobles and landholders did not want to be associated with a Scottish defeat against Edward. This was a heavy blow for Wallace, as his archers were now left unprotected. This demonstrated that the nobility were not willing to commit completely to what seemed like a futile resistance.

Edward I changed his tactics and instead picked off the men in the schiltrons with volleys of arrows from his Welsh longbowmen. The schiltron pikes were dug into the ground. This gave them more stability; however, it also made them immobile and the men inside were unable to avoid the hails of arrows, which slaughtered them where they stood. The Scottish archers were also cut down as they had no cavalry left to protect them. All who did not flee into Callander Wood were killed by the English cavalry. Roughly a third of the Scottish army was killed, with only 110 horse and 2,000 infantry killed on the English side.

The victory for Edward I was welcomed by the English nobility, and English garrisons were slowly re-established in castles south of the Forth. Edward marched to Stirling, restored the castle to his command, then he went west to Ayr to wait for supply ships. These never came and his forces were forced to march south to Dumfries before taking Lochmaben Castle in Annandale. Edward added **peels** to the castles of Dumfries and Selkirk and then organised supplies and garrisons to be sent around Berwick, Edinburgh, Stirling, Roxburgh and Jedburgh. However, lack of food forced the army south to Carlisle in September.

All this meant that the Battle of Falkirk did not have the same result on Scotland as Dunbar in 1296. In fact, Edward would not have this level of control again until the winter of 1303–04. For now, Edward I controlled Scotland as far as Stirling Castle, and a small way into Lochmaben but no further. This meant that large parts of Scotland were governed by Guardians in the name of King John Balliol and the Scots were able to continue their resistance. They had also learnt lessons from Falkirk and swapped their tactics to guerrilla warfare. They would not attempt another **pitched battle** against Edward again until 1314, 16 years later.

The defeat at Falkirk also had an impact on the middling folk of Scotland, who had fought for Wallace. Some people had chosen to support Wallace against the wishes of their lord. After the Battle of Falkirk, dozens of farmers and their heirs are listed as being deprived of their lands because they had fought for Wallace. This suggests that the middling folk in Scotland faced significant economic and social consequences from the Falkirk defeat.

The Battle of Falkirk was a disaster for Wallace, ending his spell as Guardian. Despite this, Scotland continued to be governed by Guardians in the name of King John Balliol. For example, in 1301 John Soules was appointed Guardian directly by John Balliol, who was still in exile. The last Guardian, John Comyn, governed the Kingdom of Scotland until 9 February 1304 – the end of John Balliol's reign.

Continuing Scottish resistance

A parliament was held sometime before December 1298, after Edward I's army was forced to retreat south to avoid hunger. Wallace was removed from the Guardianship due to his loss of Falkirk. Two new Guardians of Scotland were appointed: Robert Bruce VII, the Earl of Carrick, and John Comyn the Younger of Badenoch. The defeat at Falkirk and the silence from Rome signalled to some that God was not on the side of John Balliol, despite the fact that most of Scotland remained in Scottish control. The Guardianship was a form of compromise between the Scottish magnates. It gave the Comyns and the Bruces, both families that had historical claims to the throne, a stake in the government of Scotland. However, Bruce worked with Comyn only until 1300, when it became clear that there was a possibility of John Balliol being reinstated as King. Despite this, the continuation of the Guardianship between 1297 and 1304 demonstrates that the Scottish resistance against Edward I would and could continue, at least north of the Forth, despite aggression from Edward's forces. The Scottish nobility of the Bruces and the Comyns were, for the moment, able to work together for their mutual goal of removing English control.

However, on 19 August 1299 a council was held in Selkirk Forest. Here, Bruce VII and Comyn clashed over whether or not Wallace's lands should be removed from him. The result was the appointment of Bishop Lamberton as third Guardian to mediate between the existing two. It is clear that, while the Guardianship was intact, it was a very shaky agreement. By 1300 Bruce had resigned from the Guardianship and changed sides to fight for Edward I.

Edward I planned to continue his fight into Scotland in 1299. However, his marriage to Margaret, the daughter of the King of France, was to be a major state occasion and required planning that could not be distracted by a campaign north of the border. Also, although Edward had granted many lands in Scotland to his nobility, such as the lands of James Stewart to the Earl of Lincoln, this had done little to smooth over tensions from the previous year. The delay allowed the Scottish forces to consolidate and maintain their campaign in Scotland.

They continued to resist Edward I in two ways. First, they put pressure on English castle garrisons, circling them and trying to cut them off from their supplies. They also carried out economic raids aimed at terrifying and impoverishing the populations that supported the English garrisons. For example, by the summer of 1299, raiders were able to cut the supply lines which supported Stirling Castle and its garrison so the castle inhabitants began to starve. By November, the garrison had surrendered. This was a major strategic prize that gave the Scottish resistance access to far more land, food and men, which strengthened its position greatly.

Although Edward I tried to retaliate by summoning 16,000 men to Berwick in mid-December, only 2,500 arrived and he was not able to launch his campaign.

In June 1298, Bishop Lamberton was in Rome and then France, trying to convince the French King and Pope Boniface VIII to write to Edward I and demand the freedom of the Scottish King. On 7 July 1299, a letter to Edward arrived from Rome demanding the immediate release of both the King and any members of the Scottish Church who were imprisoned. Boniface's letter told Edward to send Balliol to Rome, where he would be maintained by the Vatican. The letter meant that the staunch supporter of an independent Scotland, Bishop Wishart, would be freed from Roxburgh. The letter was supported by the demand from King Philip of France, who made the release of Balliol a part of his peace deal with England along with Edward's marriage to Philip's sister, Margaret. Balliol was released from Edward's custody on 18 July 1299. He was caught at Dover trying to smuggle out the Great Seal and the gold crown of Scotland, perhaps intent on using them again. He was moved to exile in the Bishop of Cambrai's castle of Malmaison in northern France. This put significant pressure on Edward and was a victory for the Scottish resistance as it put them one step closer to reinstating Balliol.

Furthermore, in June 1299 Pope Boniface VIII issued a papal bull to Edward I. The letter stated that Edward should not be invading Scotland and demanded that Edward send proof of the legality of his conquest in Scotland to Rome for permission to continue. The letter claimed that 'from ancient times the realm of Scotland belonged rightfully, and is known still to belong, to the Roman Church'. It also reminded Edward that the negotiations at Birgham had promised that Scotland would maintain its independence. Scotland had received the title of Rome's special daughter in the years before the Great Cause, and the letter accused Edward of taking advantage of the country while it was in an unstable position. This bull was no doubt the result of Scottish petitioning at the papal court. It delayed Edward's efforts in Scotland as he made a truce with the Guardians until May 1301. Arguably, this delay favoured Edward more than it did the Guardians, however, as it prevented the Guardians from taking back the gains in land that Edward had made.

From July 1301, the fighting recommenced with a two-pronged attack from Edward I and his 17-year-old son, Edward II. The castles of Bothwell in Glasgow and Stonehouse first fell to the English army and then were retaken by Scottish forces. The then Guardians, John Comyn and John Soules, refused to fight the English army head on but rather removed their army to the north until the English were forced to retreat for winter. The Battle of Roslin in February 1303 saw a Comyn army wipe out an English force during a night raid and the Guardians continued to resist Edward I's men as best they could. At some point in 1303, they were rejoined by William Wallace (but not as Guardian).

England and France signed the Treaty of Asnières on 26 January 1302. The treaty stated that Edward I had to hand over all the land taken in Scotland since the start of his campaign there in 1301 to the French. This included the strongholds of Bothwell and Turnberry. The peace also demanded the granting of a truce with Scotland until 1 November 1302. Edward returned to England in February 1303. This was a small victory for the Scottish resistance; however, it also signalled the end of French help to restore Balliol to the throne. Balliol would remain in France until he died and never would return to Scotland to become King. He had lost all his lands in England and lived the rest of his life on his family estates in Bailleul in France. He died in his family chateau at Hélicourt in France in late 1314, aged around 65. He was, however, survived by his son Edward Balliol, who would later inherit his claim to the throne and become King of Scots.

Between 1303 and 1304, Edward I mounted his final attack in Scotland. He floated his own pontoon up the Forth so he could cross at Stirling, as the bridge still had not been fixed since 1297. He crossed the Forth on 10 June 1303 and made it as far north as Aberdeen. Edward even stayed in Comyn's island fortress of Lochindorb to insult the leader and show him who really had power. Although the English army was struggling to feed itself, Edward wintered in Scotland at Dunfermline Abbey from November. Scottish forces still held Stirling Castle, but this was a much more powerful attack than before. Edward's reconquest of Scotland was complete when Stirling Castle finally fell to him in July 1304.

Edward I sent messengers requesting negotiation north to the Guardians from late December. Finally, on 11 January 1304, Edward's negotiators went to Kinclaven royal castle on the River Tay to discuss a peace deal with Comyn. On 8 February, Edward agreed the negotiated terms of surrender, and Comyn then surrendered at Strathord on 9 February. Comyn swore a homage of fealty to Edward a week later, on 16 February, as a result of this surrender. The Scots were to swear homage and fealty to Edward again. Edward was granted permission to impose penalties on those who had fought against him and could distribute land in Scotland how he wanted. However, unlike the defeat of Dunbar, it was made clear that the Scots had not been beaten and had put up a good fight. No Scots, bar Wallace, were to be executed or face physical harm for their part in the uprising against Edward. This was the end of the Scottish resistance in Scotland for the time being. It is said that on 21 February Edward joined John Comyn and his knights in a feast of herring, stockfish and wine.

Wallace had been in Europe since 1299 trying to convince the Pope and the French King to send John Balliol back to Scotland to claim his land. He fought on the side of the Guardians when he returned to Scotland. In June 1303, Wallace had helped to lead an army through Caerlaverock and Dumfries, before marching through Annandale to join Sir Simon Fraser's raid in Carlisle. They harassed the area to prevent supplies from reaching the English garrisons in the south-west. Edward I sent part of his army, led by the royal lieutenant Sir Aymer de Valence, who was also the Guardian Comyn's brother-in-law, to quell the threat. In this way, Wallace never gave up the Scottish resistance and the fight to reinstate John Balliol to the throne.

Wallace was the only person in Scotland who did not receive a pardon from Edward I under the terms of his 1304 settlement. In August 1305, Wallace was captured by Sir John Menteith in Glasgow and handed over to Edward for trial. This marked the end of Wallace's resistance in Scotland; he had been surrendered by men he had once led, men who probably saw him by then as a barrier to peace with Edward.

Wallace was taken to London where he was placed on a show trial. His charges were read to him and, as a man of low rank, he was not allowed to respond or defend himself. In some ways, trying to offer a defence would have been to recognise that Edward I had a right to try him for treason, which Wallace's supporters said he did not. This was because Wallace had never sworn an oath of loyalty to Edward. The point of the trial was to demonstrate Edward's authority and show that Scottish resistance was over.

William Wallace was executed on 23 August 1305 as part of the entertainment at the St Bartholomew Fair. Public execution was a matter of course in England but ritualistic killings were not common and would provide entertainment for the Londoners. Wallace was taken from the Tower of London to Aldgate and then to Smithfield where he was dragged for nearly 4 miles through the streets behind a horse, which would have been a slow and painful journey. The 'drawing' probably took at least two hours, if not longer, as the streets would have been busy, and Wallace would have been wrapped in hide to make sure he was alive when he reached the execution site. He was then hanged by the neck. While he was still alive, the executioners cut his torso open so that his organs could be removed and burned in front of him. Finally, Wallace's head was chopped off and placed on a spike on London Bridge. His body was quartered, with one piece each going to Berwick, Perth and Stirling as a warning to others who dared resist Edward I's rule. The other piece was sent to Newcastle as a trophy for the city's suffering at the hands of Wallace. It is clear that Edward wanted to obliterate Wallace's image completely. Certainly, Edward had been forced to offer very lenient terms to the Scottish nobility in their surrender, and it was important that he did not look weak. Wallace acted as a sort of scapegoat, to make a spectacle of Edward's strength, without the consequence of any retaliation from the noble families of Scotland.

Figure 3.8 A memorial to Wallace on St Bartholomew's Hospital, Smithfield, which is close to the spot where Wallace was executed in 1305.

Although Wallace had not succeeded in his mission to restore Balliol, Wallace and the Guardian regime had managed to prevent Edward I's annexation of Scotland for eight years between 1296 and 1304. He also managed to evade capture for eight months after he was outlawed, suggesting he still had sympathisers in Scotland.

ACTIVITIES

1. Create a timeline of William Wallace's life, from the beginning of his resistance to his execution in 1305. Try to find at least ten points to put on your timeline.
2. Although Wallace was important in the Scottish Wars of Independence, he was not the only person involved. Pick the five most important people in this chapter, aside from Wallace, and create a fact file for each of them. You should include:
   a. their name
   b. where they were from
   c. their job role
   d. any other information about them.
3. For some, William Wallace is considered a freedom fighter and, for others, he is considered a terrorist. Make a table, like the one below, and add evidence to support both points of view.

Evidence Wallace was a freedom fighter	Evidence Wallace was a terrorist

4. Create a PowerPoint presentation about the period between 1297 and 1305. You should include ten events that were important to the fight for Scottish resistance. Use no fewer than three images and no more than 20 words on each slide to explain the role of William Wallace in the Scottish resistance.

GLOSSARY

Term	Meaning
aristocracy	The highest class of people in society, made up of people of noble birth who hold hereditary titles and offices.
esquire	A young nobleman who, in training for knighthood, acted as an attendant to a knight.
flay	To strip the skin off a corpse or carcass.
guerrilla	A type of warfare that aims to avoid head-on confrontations with enemy armies, by engaging in small, surprise skirmishes with the goal of exhausting the opponents and forcing them to withdraw.
magnate	A particularly powerful noble who is lord of large areas of the country.
middling folk	People who are between nobles and serfs in status. They formed the infantry core of the Scottish 'common army'.
muster	To assemble (troops), especially for inspection or in preparation for battle.
peel	A small fortified tower built for defence.
pitched battle	A battle in which the time and place are determined beforehand, rather than a casual or chance skirmish.
raise the standard	To take up arms or prepare to fight.
schiltron	A compact body of troops forming a battle array, shield wall or phalanx. The term is most often associated with Scottish pike formations during the Wars of Scottish Independence in the late thirteenth and early fourteenth centuries.
treason	A crime against the King personally.

Chapter 4

The rise and triumph of Robert Bruce VII

The aim of this chapter is to examine the rise and triumph of Robert Bruce VII between 1306 and 1328.

LINK TO EXAM

Higher

Key issue 4: An evaluation of the reasons for the rise and triumph of Robert Bruce VII

Background

Robert Bruce VII was born to Robert Bruce VI and Marjory of Carrick on 11 July 1274. The Bruces were a powerful noble family that ruled Annandale and Carrick in the south-west of Scotland. There has been a significant amount of research done about Robert Bruce VII. The first work of length was written by John Barbour in 1375. This was a long narrative poem called 'The Brus', which tells the story of his actions. Much like Blind Harry's 'Wallace', Barbour's tale needs to be understood alongside other evidence and more recent historical research.

On Thursday, 11 June 1304, Robert Bruce VII met with Bishop Lamberton of St Andrews. Bishops held one of the most important roles in Scotland because they connected the Church, and therefore its people, to the Pope in Rome and thereafter to God. Lamberton had been a Guardian with Bruce and had been key in negotiations to secure the release of John Balliol from Edward I. The pair met at Cambuskenneth Abbey. They made a secret pact stating that they would support each other against all others, no matter what the cost. The penalty for breaking the agreement was £10,000, a huge sum of money for such an alliance. Lamberton had sworn an oath of allegiance to Edward of England only two months before, and Bruce had voluntarily joined Edward's army to fight in Scotland in 1302. Bruce had also helped Edward I transport siege equipment to Stirling: both Bruce and Lamberton were biding their time. This deal made it clear that this fealty with Edward was temporary. Although there is no specific evidence of what their actions were to be, the historian G. Barrow suggests it is most likely, considering the sums of money involved, that this was an acknowledgement that the future of independent Scotland lay with Bruce. This agreement was made during Edward's siege of Stirling Castle, the last outpost of resistance.

At the very moment that Edward was on the verge of complete victory in Scotland, and within sight of Stirling Castle, the seeds were being sown of the next rising. Crucially, Lamberton recognised that the cause of Balliol was lost and the only hope of independence was through Bruce.

However, on the surface, Bruce VII was Edward I's close ally. He was made the sheriff of Lanark and Ayr, and earned an impressive income from his lands in Carrick and Annandale in Scotland, Hatfield and Writtle in Essex, Tottenham in Middlesex and Caldecot in Huntingdon.

The rise and triumph of Robert Bruce VII

For the exam, it is important to understand the reasons for the rise and triumph of Robert Bruce VII. This chapter will examine the ambitions of Bruce and consider his conflict and victory over his Scottish opponents. It will then consider his victory at Bannockburn and its impact after 1314. Next, it will examine the period of continuing hostilities until 1328, as Robert Bruce formed his new government and ran Scotland as its King. Finally, it will consider the Declaration of Arbroath and the Treaties of Edinburgh and Northampton in 1328.

The discussion in this chapter will be divided into the following areas:

- 4.1 The ambitions of Robert Bruce VII:
    - Bruce's conflict with and victory over Scottish opponents, 1306–14
    - Bruce's victory at Bannockburn
- 4.2 Continuing hostilities, 1314–28
- 4.3 The Declaration of Arbroath, 6 April 1320
- 4.4 The Treaties of Edinburgh/Northampton, 1328

4.1 The ambitions of Robert Bruce VII

Since the death of Alexander III, Scotland had been without a stable monarch. John Balliol had fled to France and any hope of his return had dissipated by 1302. During this time, Scotland had been run by a number of Guardians who served the community of the realm. John Comyn of Badenoch, head of the powerful Comyn family and Guardian from 1298, had essentially been running the kingdom of Scotland in the absence of a monarch and was responsible to Edward I. However, by 1305, Edward was in his mid-60s, elderly by medieval standards. The place of the kingdom of Scotland in relation to that of England was likely on the minds of the senior members of the Scottish nobility, especially given that Edward II would soon replace his father. Bruce and Comyn both had claims to the throne through their connection to David, Earl of Huntington. However, Comyn was also the nephew to the recently exiled Balliol. This made him the most likely man to be chosen as King when Edward I died. Compared to Bruce, Comyn was a highly experienced warlord and controlled large areas of the country. Bruce, although an earl, commanded smaller areas of land, but he had voluntarily fought for Edward I from 1302 and had acquired some experience and understanding of Edward's war machine. Edward's peace with Scotland had left the Comyns with significant power. They still retained their land, and many of their men held important positions in Edward's government of occupation. Both Bruce and Comyn were members of the council appointed in 1305 to advise Edward's lieutenant.

In order to become King, Bruce VII would have to deal first with his domestic opposition. The fight for sovereignty was, essentially, a civil war.

Figure 4.1 Some of the major towns of Scotland.

Bruce's conflict with and victory over Scottish opponents, 1306–14

On 10 February 1306 at Greyfriars Church in Dumfries, Robert Bruce VII met with Sir John Comyn. Comyn had been at his castle in Dalswinton, about 7 miles north of Dumfries, and Bruce asked to see him. The church was probably considered neutral ground: necessary as these two men did not have a history of good relations. It is clear that Comyn did not feel threatened by Bruce, as he was not wearing armour and came with only two men to support him: his valet Richard Galbraith and his uncle, Robert Balliol. Bruce arrived with four men: Alexander Lindsey, his close friend, and the three Seton brothers, who had been loyal Scottish supporters during the resistance of 1298. Bruce arrived in armour.

Although historians do not know exactly what happened, there was an altercation and arguing during which Bruce VII stabbed John Comyn, killing him. Anti-Bruce propaganda tells that Comyn was murdered on the altar by Bruce's hand. Pro-Bruce propaganda tells us that the murder was not premeditated and happened in the heat of the moment. These chronicles suggest that Bruce's men came back into the church to ensure that Comyn was dead. By doing this, they cast doubt on whether Bruce should be held ultimately responsible.

The fact remained that Sir John Comyn, the leader of the hugely powerful Comyn family, who would very likely have put himself forward as King of Scotland upon Edward I's death, had been killed.

This act had serious consequences for Bruce VII's rise to power. He had now successfully removed his biggest political rival from any possible future claim to be King and also removed demands for a Balliol restoration. However, he now had the entire force of the Comyn families and their allies against him for killing one of their own. The murder also angered Edward I, as Bruce should have been supporting Edward's government in Scotland. Ten days after the murder, Edward I began making plans to return to Scotland to put an end to Bruce's uprising.

Figure 4.2 John Comyn is killed by Robert Bruce VII before the high altar of the Greyfriars Church in Dumfries, 1306, as portrayed by Felix Phillippoteaux, a nineteenth-century French illustrator. It is important to note that Phillippoteaux may have had his own biases about how Comyn was murdered, which can be seen reflected in this illustration.

Murder in a church was considered **sacrilegious** as a church was seen as holy ground. Therefore, the murder meant that Bruce VII risked being **excommunicated** from the Catholic Church of Rome. Excommunication would mean he would be unable to be King as he could not participate in the religious sacraments. Although his biggest rival was removed, murder put him in an unfavourable position against his Scottish opponents.

Immediately after the murder, Bruce VII and his men captured Dumfries Castle. There, they met with more supporters and continued on to the royal castle at Ayr and then Inverkip. In the islands, Bruce's men took Rothesay Castle on Bute, Dunaverty Castle on Kintyre and reinforced Bruce's Loch Doon Castle in Carrick. These castles were strategically important for Bruce's early campaign because taking them removed his opponents' power in the area and also gave him access to sea routes into the west of Scotland. It is clear these actions were intentional and planned, not forced by a quick decision. This implies Bruce's actions at Greyfriars Church had not been an unplanned reaction to a fight. It was important that Bruce acted quickly to establish a strategic power base.

Bruce VII then met with Bishop Wishart of Glasgow on Saturday, 5 March. Wishart agreed that Bruce should attempt to claim the crown of Scotland himself and forgave Bruce for his sacrilegious crimes. This forgiveness was very important because the probability of excommunication still loomed and an excommunicated King could not rule. The support that Wishart gave Bruce in his efforts to become King would be powerful both spiritually and politically. However, it should be noted that this decision was not supported by the Pope in Rome.

From his meeting with Wishart, Bruce VII travelled north to Scone. He had been given robes suitable for the event by Wishart and sent a banner with the royal coat of arms that Wishart had been hiding. On 25 March 1306, Bruce was inaugurated King of Scots at the palace of Scone. Bishop Lamberton arrived two days later to conduct mass on 27 March, also Palm Sunday. This served to strengthen his position. Once inaugurated, Bruce's campaign acquired the legitimacy from the Scottish clergy that it needed to bring some other Scottish nobles and previous opponents onto his side.

Isabella, the Countess of Buchan, enthroned Bruce VII. She was daughter of the Earl of Fife and this was her family's traditional role in Scottish inaugurations. This was an immense personal sacrifice for her as she was married to the murdered Comyn's cousin, John Comyn, Earl of Buchan. Importantly, Lamberton and Isabella gave the ceremony the credibility it needed. However, the inauguration was not well attended, with the Earls of Fife and Strathearn missing. These families traditionally led the man who was going to be inaugurated to the throne. However, the Earls of Mar, Atholl, Lennox and Menteith were probably in attendance, although this was a minority of the nobility. This implies that Bruce's inauguration was not supported by all the magnates in Scotland, revealing both how politically divided Scotland was and how far Bruce was going to have to go to get the country to support his kingship.

Despite this, the inauguration allowed Bruce VII to begin to collect royal rent to fund his campaign. After the inauguration, he rode to gather supporters between Perth, Dundee, Forfar and Aberdeen. In Perth he collected £54 of 'royal rent', a large sum at that time. He also drew a small fighting force from the 'middling folk', who had endured almost ten years of Edward I's overlordship and subjugation. Finally, he forced some of the Scottish lords to swear fealty to him, the highest profile of these being the Earl of Strathearn, John Comyn of Buchan's brother-in-law. This all allowed him to fund and legitimise his campaign in the eyes of the other nobility in Scotland, although there were many who still questioned his legitimacy as King.

However, after the inauguration, Edward I retaliated quickly. It would normally have taken a couple of weeks, or maybe even a month, to mobilise an army in England at that time. However, Sir Aymer de Valence was sent to put down the Bruce revolt on 5 April 1306, less than two weeks after Bruce VII was inaugurated. It is fair to say that Edward was enraged at the audacity of Bruce turning against him and claiming the throne. In reaction Edward 'raised the dragon', a banner that removed all chivalric code from conflict and demonstrated that no mercy would be shown, regardless of rank. As far as Edward was concerned, Bruce and his supporters were being ungrateful for the generous peace he had offered them in 1305. This quick mobilisation of his troops was highly important as it forced the Scottish nobility to pick a side. They had to choose whether to fight with Edward against Bruce, or fight alongside Bruce's new government. This galvanised some nobles who did not want English overlordship to support Bruce.

Bruce VII faced a number of early defeats at the hands of Edward I's troops, Edward's Scottish supporters and rival Scottish nobles. The first of Bruce's major conflicts was the Battle of Methven Wood. Valence had come across the border on 22 May with an army of 4,500 horses, 140 crossbowmen and 2,000 foot soldiers. He had been given orders from Edward to burn and destroy the lands of those who supported Bruce. Bruce met Valence at Perth, which Bruce had occupied. Bruce and his supporters came dressed in white linen to avoid being identified and facing the wrath of the dragon banner. Valence tricked Bruce. He told Bruce that he would not fight him that day, because it was a feast day, and agreed to leave the castle walls the next morning. Bruce retreated to Methven Wood for the evening to take shelter and feed his men. However, this was a deception and, instead, Valence routed Bruce's men that night. They were surprised by the attack and Bruce was fortunate to escape.

This was a major blow for the new King and was a great defeat in his early campaign against both Edward I and Edward's Scottish allies as he lost important military commanders and men. For example, Sir Thomas Randolph, one of Bruce VII's long-time supporters and an able commander, was captured, and on 4 August, 16 of Bruce's other men were hanged. Two of these men were knights and it would have been shocking for them to be treated like common criminals in their execution. The Battle of Methven Wood seriously reduced Bruce's fighting force and significantly weakened his attempt to assert himself as King of Scots.

Edward I's forces had captured both Bishop Wishart and Bishop Lamberton by 9 June 1306. This was another blow to Bruce VII's attempt to triumph as King in Scotland as these two members of the clergy had been vital in giving him guidance and legitimising his claim to the throne. Without them, his ability to solidify his claim in the eyes of the Scottish Church was in jeopardy.

The second of Bruce VII's early conflicts was the Battle of Dalrigh. On 11 August 1306, Bruce crossed paths with John MacDougall of Lorne at Dalrigh, the route to the west. The MacDougalls had been some of the first resisters of Edward I's regime in 1296; however, they were blood relatives of the murdered Comyn. This meant they were now sworn enemies of Bruce. When the two sides met, the MacDougalls dismounted their horses and sliced at the backs of Bruce's men's horses and their riders with their axes, forcing the group to scatter and flee. This defeat was important because it confirmed that many Scots did not support Bruce or the idea of him becoming King of Scots. Some even felt that these early defeats were evidence that God had abandoned Bruce. Bruce only just escaped with his life and some of his supporters, such as Sir Simon Fraser, left his side so his force was further weakened. It is estimated that, after this second defeat, his force had been reduced to only to a few men. Fraser was caught and hanged, drawn and quartered around 7 September, and his head was placed on a spike next to Wallace's on the Tower of London.

Bruce VII was forced northwards where he, his remaining supporters and his family had to survive by hunting and fishing to catch pike, salmon, trout and eel. To try to protect the future of his dynasty, Bruce sent the women in the party – his teenage second wife, Elizabeth, and his daughter, Marjorie – 40 miles away into the care of his brother Neil Bruce at the stronghold of Kildrummy Castle in Mar. However, soon after they left, Bruce learned that Prince Edward II was heading to Kildrummy to try to capture the women as hostages. Bruce sent the Earl of Atholl to tell his brother, Neil Bruce, to take the women from the castle and leave Scotland altogether. Ideally, they were to take refuge with their sister Isobel Bruce, the Queen of Norway, in Norway.

Although they got to the coast and boarded a ship, bad weather meant it did not set sail and they were captured at St Duthac's church in Tain by Edward II and his force. Elizabeth was treated relatively well, as she was the daughter of the Earl of Ulster. She was kept in Burstwick near Yorkshire, in the company of women who Edward apparently said should 'not be merry at all'. Marjorie was to be locked in a cage in the Tower of London at first, before being sent to a convent at Watton. Christian, Bruce VII's sister, was sent to a convent in Sixhills in Lincolnshire, and his other sister, Mary, was locked in a special cage Edward built for her, inside Roxburgh Castle. Isabella of Fife, who had inaugurated the King, was also built a cage in the tower of Berwick Castle and only allowed to talk to the two English women who gave her food. They would all remain in captivity until after Bannockburn in 1314. This both demonstrated Edward's ferocity and acted as a major setback for Bruce, as he needed his Queen and his daughter to continue his dynasty and secure his crown. Without a credible heir, Bruce was more likely to be assassinated by his opponents.

Other important members of Bruce VII's party were also captured around this time. The three Seton brothers, Sir Christopher Seton, John Seton and Humphry Seton, who had retreated to the safety of Bruce's Carrick Castle near Loch Doon, were all caught by Edward II when he besieged the castle in August 1306. The castle fell after just a week as its keeper, the Governor Sir Gilbert de Carrick, feared Bruce was dead and so did not put up a fight. This was a huge blow for Bruce's attempt to secure the Scottish crown. The Seton brothers were all hanged, drawn and quartered for their part in Comyn's murder. Bruce now no longer had control of his family estate and so had no safe stronghold to which to return to regroup.

By the end of August 1306, the Bruce campaign was in real peril and rumours of Bruce VII's death circulated around Scotland. With the help of boats from the Earl of Lennox, Bruce travelled from Loch Lomond to the south of Kintyre, where he planned on wintering at Dunaverty Castle. However, he was quickly followed by an English army led by Henry Percy. Percy's troops besieged the castle for six weeks before it fell. Bruce had travelled to Islay and then been blown south by the wind to Rathlin. Rathlin was owned by his father-in-law, Richard, Earl of Ulster, who, as the father of his captured wife, would be likely to hand Bruce over to Edward I. From here, Bruce's whereabouts were unknown until he returned in the spring of 1307. This meant that the winter of 1306–07 marked the lowest point in his campaign to secure the throne as he had few supporters, no army and did not know whom he could trust on the mainland. He was forced into hiding, and it is likely that the magnates of Scotland and Edward I thought they had heard the last of Bruce.

However, it is also likely that Bruce VII still had some money, as some of his men were sent to collect rents from his earldom in Carrick during the winter. Michael Penman suggests that he was probably with '**kindred**' and allies in Ireland. Here, Bruce must have made plans for his return to Scotland.

Bruce VII returned to Scotland in early February 1307. Historian F. Watson argues that it is likely that sympathetic Irish families, such as the O'Neils of Tyrone, the O'Connors of Connacht and the O'Donnells of Donegal, provided him with boats and some men with which to return. Two of his brothers, Thomas and Alexander, were the first to land in Scotland. They landed at Loch Ryan and were intercepted by Sir Dougall MacDowel, a member of a leading Galloway family. The brothers had intended to raid Galloway with 300 Scots and 700 Irish auxiliaries. However, they were quickly crushed by a MacDowel force, which captured both brothers. They were immediately delivered to Edward VII, who was near Carlisle, and were executed. Thomas was hanged, drawn and quartered. This was an early blow for Bruce's comeback, losing not only more brothers but able leaders. However, his fortunes were about to change.

Bruce VII now employed guerrilla warfare, hit-and-run tactics, rather than trying to hold any pitched battle against his opponents. His army was small, and these tactics gave him an advantage against larger, more organised forces. His first victory was at Glen Trool. Although no records survive of the event, according to Barbour's poem 'The Brus', Bruce was followed by Valence and Clifford, who had over 1,500 men compared to Bruce's 300, for three weeks. The two armies met in a narrow pass at the eastern end of Loch Trool, near Glen Trool. This was not suitable for Valence's mounted knights, forcing them off their horses and into a single-file march with the loch on one side and a steep slope on the other. Bruce's army had a high position up the steep slope, known as the Steps of Trool. They rolled boulders, hurled rocks and fired arrows on the enemy below them. Bruce's army then charged and split the force in half to prevent them manoeuvring, cutting them down with heavy losses. This was a small but very important victory for Bruce. It encouraged men to join his army and provided a much-needed confidence boost for his campaign. Many Scots believed that victories demonstrated that God was on the side of the winner. So, this victory would have spiritually encouraged his men too.

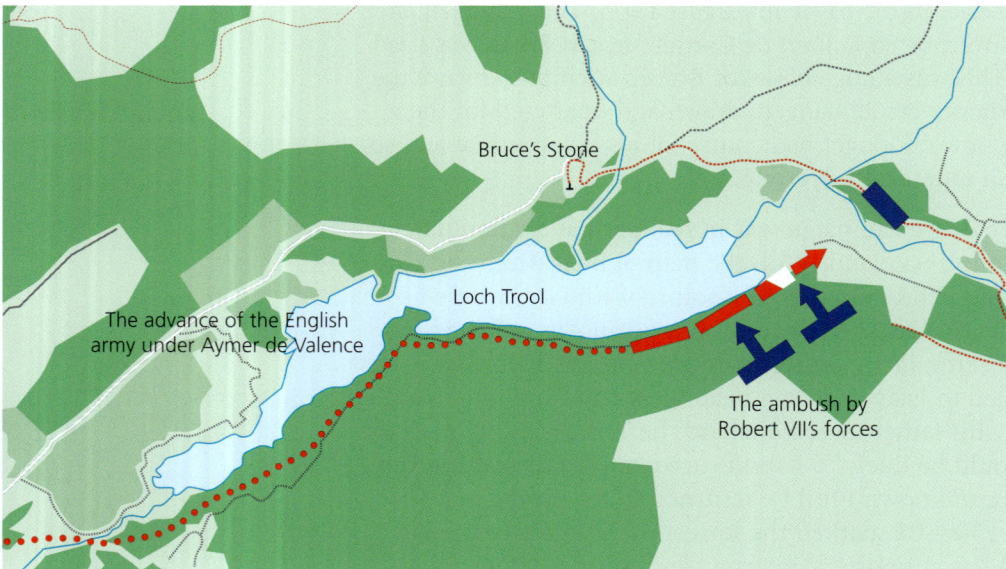

Figure 4.3 The Battle of Glen Trool on Loch Trool.

Bruce VII's next victory was the Battle of Loudon Hill on 10 May 1307. After Glen Trool, Bruce made his way quickly over the hills of Ayrshire. He organised his troops on high, exposed moorland and dug trenches at right angles to the road to restrict the movement of Valence's horsemen by forcing them through in small numbers. Bruce and his brother Edward fought at the front of the 600-strong army, and they won. Bruce's forces already seemed well trained and pushed the cavalry back with their spears. Although this battle was also small in scale, its effect on Bruce's campaign to claim the throne was important for two reasons. First, it demonstrated to both his Scottish supporters and his opponents that, despite previous events, God still favoured him as he had allowed Bruce to win. Second, it proved Bruce's impressive skill and capabilities as a military leader, as it was one of the only battles won by foot soldiers against cavalry during this time (aside from Stirling Bridge). Both of these consequences brought more men to Bruce's side as it seemed more likely that his campaign would be a success.

Although not caused by battle with Bruce VII, the death of Edward I is important in understanding Bruce's rise to power. On hearing that Bruce had returned to Scotland, Edward I was incensed and decided to come to Scotland himself. However, on 7 July 1307 at Burgh on Sands near Carlisle, having failed to cross the border, Edward I died at 68 years old. Edward II, Prince of Wales and now the new King of England, remained in the north until August before abandoning the campaign in Scotland and returning south to bury his father. Edward II was **crowned** King on 25 February. This was a key moment in Bruce's struggle to come to power. Edward I was known as the 'Hammer of the Scots'. He had been a skilled politician, lawyer, tactician and adversary. His death left a power vacuum in England and in the Scottish campaign. Edward II was far less capable as he had less military experience and was politically unpopular. He continued many campaigns in Scotland, at least until 1324 but was less determined than his father had been to subdue the Scottish resistance completely. This aided Bruce's campaign against his Scottish opponents because Bruce could concentrate on fighting them instead of Edward II's forces.

Bruce VII marched north, laying siege to the stronghold of Inverlochy Castle on 25 November and taking it with the help of his supporters within the castle walls. Inverlochy was the key to the Great Glen, a natural highway to the north through the Highland mountains. Taking the castle meant that Bruce could continue his march north-east, through the Great Glen, to the lands of the powerful Comyn family. He was now joined by men from Carrick, Stewartry, Clydesdale and Lennox, as well as Irish foot soldiers. This suggests that his army had grown in size with his continued success and men began to join his campaign from all across the country.

By Christmas of 1307, Bruce VII probably carried his **galleys** between the lochs of the Great Glen to make the march north as fast as possible. The effects of Bruce VII's campaign of living on the land and engaging in guerrilla warfare were tiring his troops. They had failed to take Elgin Castle but instead had come to a truce with its garrison. Bruce also had become gravely ill and his brother, Edward Bruce, acted under orders from the King in his **litter**. This was a setback in the campaign: being sick, and having suffered a defeat, Bruce would have faced some defection from his army. There had probably been a significant amount of desertion already due to the poor conditions and the prospect of fighting in winter. His sickness made Bruce and his claim to the crown look weak to his opponents. This left him vulnerable and, in turn, left him with a less effective fighting force with which to take on his opponents.

At this time, Bruce VII's forces were located deep in hostile Comyn territory and were spotted by Earl Buchan's army in a wooded marsh near Slioch, near Huntly in Aberdeenshire. Bruce had fallen seriously ill and his brother was in charge of his army. Buchan and Atholl made an unsuccessful attack on Christmas Day; as they closed on Bruce's troops, Bruce strapped himself to his horse and rode out with his army. Buchan's troops thought that Bruce was near death and were thrown by the sight of the recognisable commander on horseback advancing towards them. This is given as one of the main reasons why both nobles and **levied, conscripted** forces fled the battleground and Bruce could claim victory. The skirmish at Slioch was immensely important in Bruce's fight for kingship. Barbour wrote in his poem 'The Brus' that, after this victory, Bruce's reputation as an extraordinary leader was solidified because he was able to inspire his troops to victory by getting on his horse despite his continued illness.

By the time Buchan's men had returned with troops on 31 December, Bruce's forces were gone, having retreated south for safety. The opposition leaders could not agree how to proceed and so did not chase Bruce VII to try to engage him in battle. That Buchan and the others were not united was important in helping Bruce win. It gave him additional time to rally and also meant he did not have to fight one of his strongest opponents in unfavourable conditions while his men were starving and weak. He was able to retreat south and return to retake the land in the spring, continuing his campaign to be recognised as King.

After making a truce with the powerful John MacDougall of Argyll, by spring of 1308 Bruce had taken many pro-Comyn castles including Inverness, Urquhart, Nairn, Balvenie, Lochindorb, Duffus, Tarradale, Skelbo and Ruthven. Bruce destroyed many of these castles because he considered them of more value to Edward II, who could use them to keep a presence in the area if he managed to return that far north, than to him, as Bruce did not need the castles to control the area because he had the support of the 'middling folk'.

This series of successes was very important in Bruce VII's rise to power as it removed many of his Scottish opponents, and it must have resulted in the number of his followers growing considerably; MacDougall wrote to Edward II on 2 June 1308 to tell him that Bruce travelled with between 10,000 and 15,000 men, all living off the land and surrounding area. While this number is probably an exaggeration, it is certain that Bruce continued to collect significant support for his campaign along the way. The size of his army now rivalled that of the northern lords and was sufficient enough to scare them into truce. Penman also notes that Bruce's success inspired spontaneous rebellion in other parts of Scotland against Bruce's opponents, the Comyn family, who were sympathetic to Edward II.

By May 1308, Bruce VII's army had marched north again to face the combined forces of John Comyn, Earl of Buchan and cousin of assassinated Guardian John Comyn of Badenoch, Duncan of Frendraught, John Mowbray and David Strathbogie. The forces met at the Battle of Barra, also known as the Battle of Inverurie, which took place on the boundary of Garioch and Buchan on 23 May 1308. Buchan drew up his forces on the road to Inverurie, between Marra Hill and Lochtern Burn and its marshes. His feudal levies were placed at the rear and his knights and men at arms were placed at the front, but his forces collapsed quickly. Bruce's men pursued Buchan and his army north to Fyvie. Bruce's success was important as it ended the active and organised resistance to his regime in Aberdeenshire.

The victory was followed by the merciless 'Herschip of Buchan'. Throughout May and June, Bruce VII's troops, under Edward Bruce, burnt land and homesteads, slaughtered livestock, destroyed grain stores and put salt and dead animals into wells, rivers and the soil to spoil them. They slaughtered those who would not submit to Bruce and razed Slains, Rattray and Dundarg Castles to the ground. The victory and the systematic destruction of the Comyn heartland, which had ruled Buchan since 1212, marked the domination of Bruce against his most powerful enemy. The wholesale devastation destroyed the Comyn power base in the north and ensured that

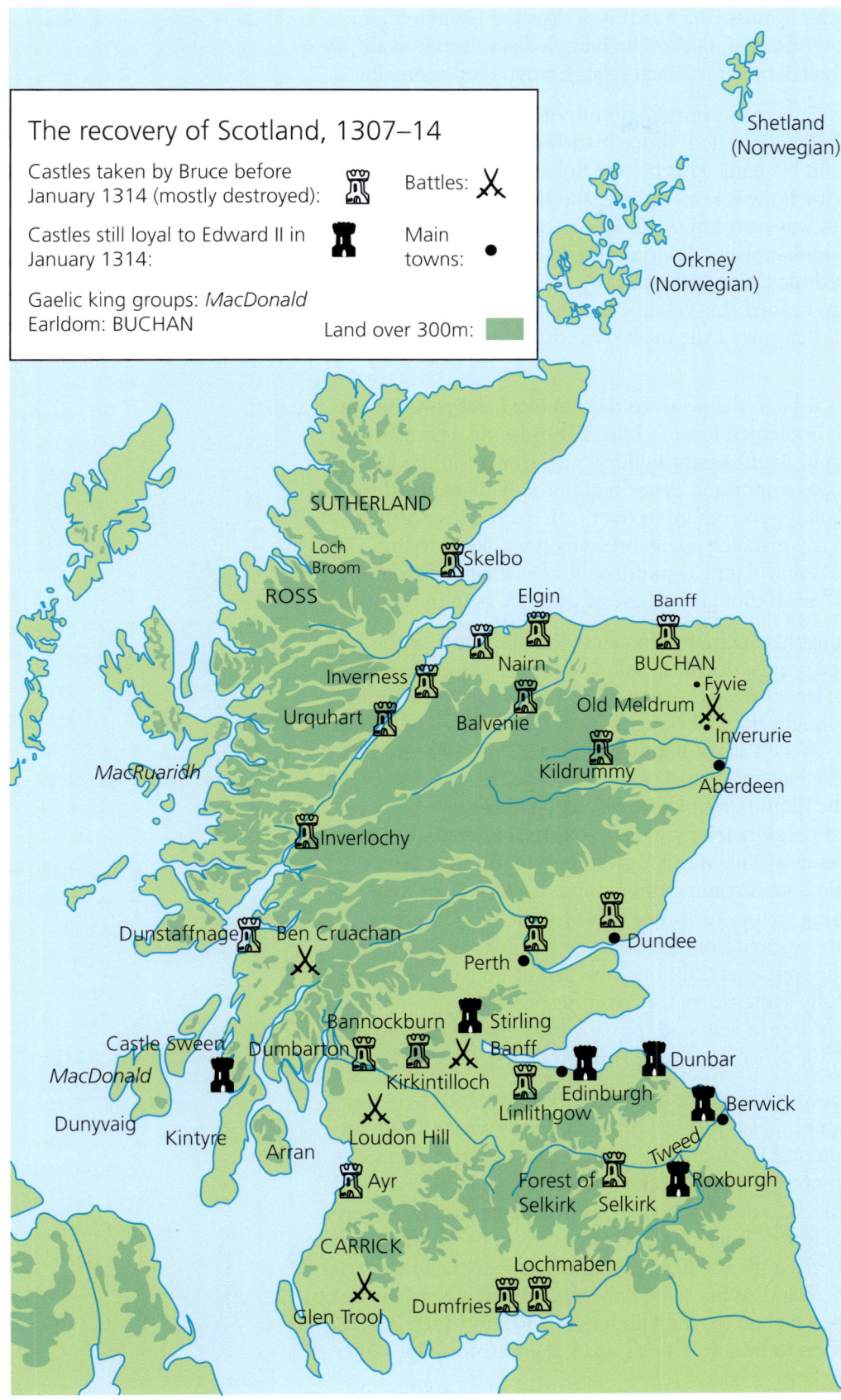

Figure 4.4 A map of Robert Bruce VII's recovery of Scotland, 1307–09. During this time Bruce won the civil war against the powerful Comyn family, who also had a claim to the throne.

there would be no more uprisings against Bruce as it was clear the Comyn regime could not protect its people. John Comyn, Earl of Buchan, fled south to Edward II's protection, removing Bruce's chief Scottish political rival. Comyn died soon after.

Additionally, the Earl of Ross, a Comyn supporter and important lord in the north, submitted to Bruce VII soon after Comyn fled. Bruce made peace with Ross, pardoned him and allowed him to maintain his land. This helped Bruce's rise to power as it gave him a powerful ally in the north who was loyal to him, and the peace was secured through marriage by 1316. Ross was now kin. Also, Ross's fealty was an important acknowledgement, from a strong Balliol and Comyn supporter, that Bruce's campaign was legitimate and he had a credible claim to the throne. The fact that Bruce accepted this truce suggests his campaign needed this validity. In other words, it was highly useful propaganda that showed that one of the most powerful Scottish nobles believed him to be King.

Finally, Bruce VII also used this time in the north to re-establish local government by giving positions of power to noblemen loyal to him. For example, Hamelin de Troup was given the sheriffdom of Banff. Restoring local government in the form of sheriffs and other landholders was important. Bruce had not only dismantled the last remnants of the Comyn–Balliol government in the north during his northern campaign, but also simultaneously installed a new one which was loyal to him. This allowed Bruce to retain political control and accumulate financial benefit from the lucrative north-east of Scotland, even though his base of power was in the south.

The final battle in his fight against his Scottish opponents was the Battle of the Pass of Brander. As Edward Bruce led a force down to Galloway, Bruce VII made his way back south through the Great Glen. During this march, sometime between 15 and 23 August 1308, Bruce's army fought the MacDougalls near Loch Awe, a fight that came to be known as the Battle of the Pass of Brander. The MacDougall army took up position on the hillside in the narrow Pass of Brander, where the River Awe cuts through the southern side of the mountain of Ben Cruachan. However, a party of Highlanders loyal to Bruce, and possibly led by James Douglas, climbed even higher up the mountain behind their enemy. The MacDougall forces found themselves trapped in the middle of Douglas's men coming down the hill and Bruce's men coming up it. This was a stunning victory for Bruce, who paraded the losers to Dunstaffnage Castle. The victory secured homage from the Lord of Argyll, one of the most powerful nobles on the west coast, although he fled to England shortly afterwards. Bruce had successfully achieved victory over his Scottish opponents and could begin to consolidate his power in Scotland, pursuing his goal of becoming internationally recognised as King of Scots.

Edward II now requested a truce with Bruce VII, between 2 February and 1 November 1309, as the English King had political problems in the south. This truce allowed Bruce to call a parliament on 31 March in St Andrews. Bruce's parliament was attended by some of the Scottish nobility. It was a time that fealties could be given and land granted to those who submitted to the new regime. The parliament at St Andrews was a powerful demonstration of Bruce's legitimacy and power in Scotland and showed both a domestic and an international audience that another government had taken over the running of the kingdom of Scotland. While King Robert I's council was still made up of some of his closest supporters, who had fought with him in 1307 and 1308, it must have had significantly more support to be able to organise local government by 1309.

Officially, the Bruce parliament had been called to discuss a letter from Philip of France, requesting that Scottish forces join a French army on crusade. In response, the parliament thanked the French King for the offer but said that Scotland had domestic issues to overcome and so was unable to join any crusade. The document stated that the 'community of the realm of Scotland' was now made up of those who swore loyalty to Robert Bruce VII as true King, so there was no need to restore Balliol. The seals of the attending nobility, and probably some who were also not in attendance, were attached to the document. It can be said that this was a powerful symbol of both Bruce's power and his acceptance in Scotland among the nobility. The correspondence helped to make the Bruce regime look more internationally respectable as it had essentially been acknowledged by another powerful monarch.

The parliament was also important because it sent a second letter, known as the Declaration of the Clergy. The Declaration of the Clergy was first issued by the Scottish clergy on 17 March 1309. The declaration was in response to Pope Clement V's summons for clergy and monarchs to attend a Church council in Vienne. The purpose of the letter was to argue that Robert Bruce VII was the true King of Scots because he was both the rightful heir to the throne by blood, and also the heir in the eyes of the people of Scotland. In other words, it claimed that the Scottish people wanted Bruce to be King because it was his birthright and because he would restore the land to its people and expel the English occupation, which was so hated. There is no doubt that this was an impressive piece of propaganda. The seals of the Bishops of Aberdeen, Argyll, Galloway and Caithness were attached to the document, though none of them were strong supporters of Bruce. Wishart was still in England so could not have attached his seal. However, real or exaggerated, this letter was important as it demonstrated that legitimacy to rule came from divine approval, the choice of the people, and military success. Military success was gained through victory in battles which, in turn, also suggested divine approval.

Bruce VII continued to secure his legitimacy by putting pressure on King Edward II to recognise Scotland as an independent kingdom, and Bruce as King. In October 1310, Edward II led an army into the kingdom of Scotland. Bruce made an eloquent appeal to Edward II, asking for peace on the understanding that Scottish independence be recognised. This previously unknown letter, written in 1310 by Bruce, was found in 2013 in a British Library manuscript. The letter seems to reveal that Bruce was willing to do anything to secure peace and independence. Equally importantly, it shows Bruce addressing Edward II in the spirit of equal kingship.

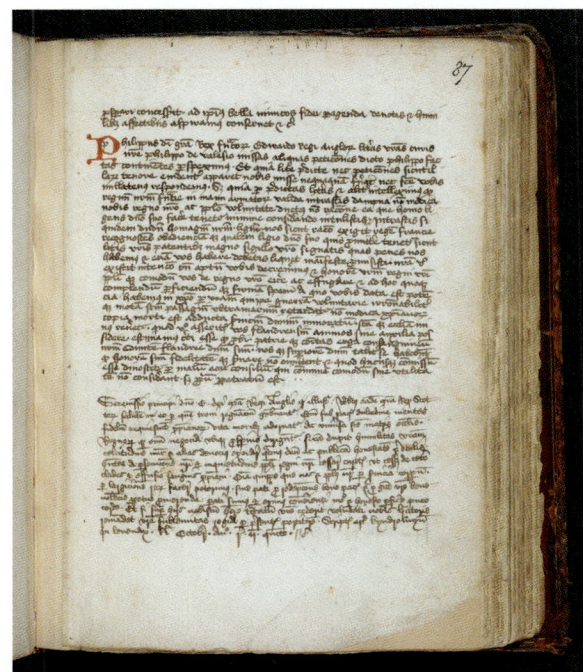

Figure 4.5 The letter of Robert Bruce VII to Edward II.

SOURCE 1

To the most serene prince the lord Edward II by God's grace illustrious King of England, Robert by the same grace King of Scots, greeting in Him through whom the thrones of those who rule are governed. ... Our humility has led us, now and at other times, to beseech your highness more earnestly so that, having God and public decency in sight, you would take pains to cease from the persecution of us and the disturbance of the people of our kingdom in order that devastation and the spilling of Christian blood may henceforth stop ...

Written at Kildrum in Lennox, the Kalends of October in the fifth year of our reign [1 October 1310].

Translation of the letter by King Robert I by Professor Dauvit Broun, University of Glasgow. The letter reveals that Bruce was willing to negotiate with Edward II, and also that he saw himself of equal rank to Edward.

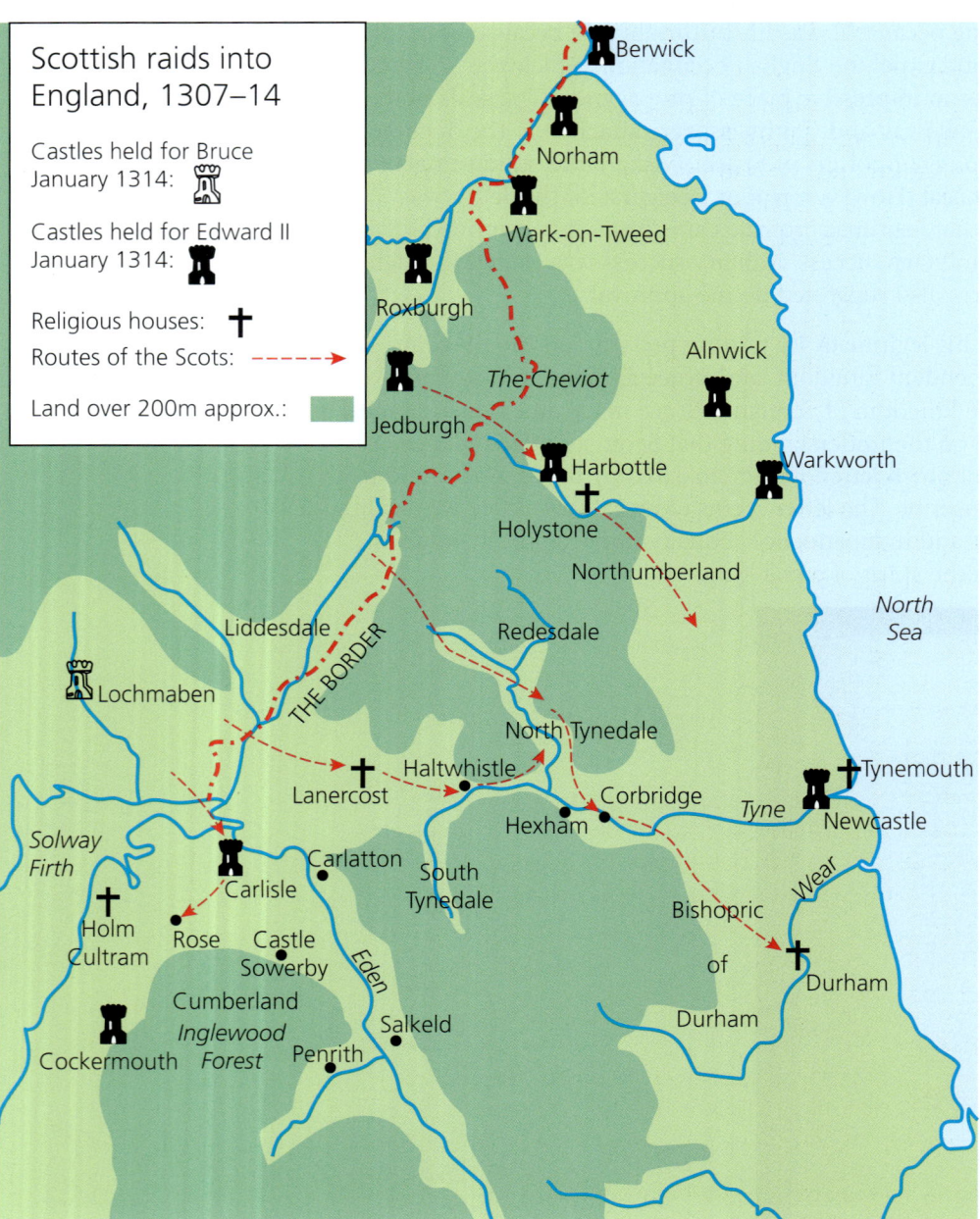

Figure 4.6 Bruce's raids into northern England between 1307 and 1314

The civil war was over and Bruce had won over most of his Scottish opponents. However, in order to be seen as King he needed Edward II to recognise him as such. Bruce led several raids into the north of England to make Edward look weak. However, he refused to commit to pitched battle. Thomas Randolph, Edward Bruce and William Douglas continued to help Bruce capture the rest of Scotland, including Dundee, Perth, Dumfries, Edinburgh and Roxburgh. By 1313, the only two castles that Bruce had not taken back were Stirling and Berwick. However, Edward II was yet to formally acknowledge Scotland's independence as a country, or Bruce as a King.

Bruce's victory at Bannockburn

Stirling Castle maintained its English garrison throughout the civil war of 1306–14. However, the garrison was fast running out of supplies due to the siege by Robert Bruce VII and his brother Edward. Edward Bruce came to an agreement with the commander of the castle, Sir Philip Mowbray, that if it had not been relieved by Midsummer's Day 1314, the fortress would be submitted to Bruce.

The Scottish army was now a well-trained, well-organised guerrilla fighting force. Bruce VII trained his men next to the River Carron, south of Stirling. Learning his lesson from Wallace at Falkirk, Bruce trained his schiltron pikemen to be offensive and mobile rather than dug into the ground. He had three schiltron formations of roughly 2,000–3,000 men, which were able to move as a unit with their long spears. This made the schiltrons significantly more effective than they had been at Falkirk because they could remain mobile, limiting their vulnerability to archers. There were also 500 cavalry under the command of Sir Robert Keith. The historian M. Penman comments that there is now a case for arguing that the Scottish army was bigger than this, with possibly between 15,000 and 20,000 men. This was highly important as it meant that the force facing Edward II at Bannockburn was a well-disciplined and well-drilled fighting force, with a great deal of military experience.

Bruce VII also chose able commanders to lead his troops. One of the schiltrons was headed by Bruce himself, another by his brother, Edward Bruce, and the third by the Earl of Moray, Thomas Randolph. There is a suggestion in Barbour's poem 'The Brus' that there was a fourth schiltron, commanded by James Douglas. However, this seems unlikely and was probably added because Douglas's family had become very powerful by the time Barbour's poem was published, so the author may have wanted to include him. Regardless, the schiltrons were clearly commanded by able and experienced men whom Bruce trusted and who had been fighting the English army since the start of his campaign, a key reason for their success.

However, Edward II had a significantly stronger army than Bruce VII. Although accounts vary, many highlight that it was at least three times larger than Bruce's. His cavalry numbers were between 2,000 and 3,000; he mustered between 15,000 and 20,000 infantry and 4,000 archers. This was, however, a smaller host than he had hoped would attend. Many of the English lords had paid 'scutage', a fee so that they did not have to provide men, instead of sending their troops to support Edward II's campaign. This played a role in Bruce's victory.

Furthermore, the English forces were not as well led as many of the previous armies that Edward I had fielded. The march north had been exhausting for them as Edward II had forced a quick march to get to Stirling in time for Midsummer's Day. This weakened his troops and reduced their morale.

Furthermore, Edward II had replaced experienced commanders with his friends, causing tension among his commanders. For example, the Earl of Hereford, whose family traditionally commanded the vanguard, was enraged when Edward II replaced him with the Earl of Gloucester, one of the King's friends. It is clear that Edward II was not the tactician his father was. He made some crucial leadership mistakes that caused much confusion and significantly weakened his army before battle even began.

The first day of the battle was Saturday, 23 June. Bruce VII had moved his troops from the woodland cover of the Torwood to a plain within the last large loop of Bannockburn, called New Park. This was a piece of firm ground, which was well defended by surrounding Coxet Hill and marshland. This strategic position forced Edward II's army to approach the battlefield via the roman road from Falkirk. This road was already narrow and Bruce had ordered his men to dig ditches filled with stakes on either side of the road to prevent the English cavalry from spreading out. A series of wet summers had also raised the water table so the ground surrounding the road was boggy. This severely weakened the advancing power of Edward's cavalry and meant Bruce had the upper hand in terms of terrain.

Edward II's army came across Bruce VII's troops and, in an attempt to win glory for himself and quickly deliver English victory, Sir Henry de Bohun, a knight in Hereford's retinue, broke from the ranks and rode directly across to Bruce, his lance pointed at the Scottish King. However, his attack missed, and as he passed, Bruce stood up in his stirrups and brought his battle-axe down on de Bohun's head, killing him. This was an enormous victory for the Scottish army and seemed to validate Bruce as rightful King, raising the morale of the Scottish troops significantly. The English army retreated and news of the event spread quickly around Edward's camp. This, in turn, significantly lowered the morale of the English troops, who were tired from their long march and interrupted night of keeping watch for Bruce's men.

A second victory of the day came when a scouting party of Edward II's, led by Clifford, was routed by the Earl of Moray's soldiers. The scouting party had been shadowing Bruce VII's forces. However, they misjudged the direction of the army and stopped too close to the trees to mount an effective charge. Moray's schiltron targeted the horses so that they would throw their riders off. Some English nobility were killed and Sir Thomas Gray was taken prisoner. The party fled back to their main camp with more stories of the Scottish victory. Again, this served to buoy the morale of Bruce's forces. Although the impact of these events is hard to quantify, it probably seemed to the Scottish army that they had a high chance of victory and that God had chosen Bruce as King.

In the evening, Bruce VII considered leaving the battlefield and retreating to his supporter the Earl of Lennox's territory for safety, as he was unsure about fighting a pitched battle against Edward II's army. However, the defection of Sir Alexander Seton from Edward's side convinced Bruce that morale in the English camp was low and that his chances of victory were high. This meant that he was convinced to fight the Battle of Bannockburn.

ACTIVITIES

1. Write a description, in no more than ten words, of the events listed below:
   a. Robert Bruce VII kills John Comyn
   b. Battle of Methven Wood
   c. Battle of Dalrigh
   d. Robert Bruce VII's flight to the Western Isles, winter 1306–07
   e. Battle of Glen Trool
   f. Battle of Loudon Hill
   g. Battle of Inverurie and the Herschip of Buchan
   h. Battle of the Pass of Brander
   i. Death of Edward I
   j. Parliament at St Andrews, 1309
   k. Battle of Bannockburn
   l. Edward II's campaign in Ireland
   m. Declaration of Arbroath
   n. Treaty of Edinburgh

2. From the list above, pick ten events that you think are the most important reasons why Robert Bruce VII was able to rise and triumph in Scotland. Draw an image to explain why each of these events mattered in his campaign.

3. The Declaration of Arbroath is an important document in Scottish history. On one hand, it signifies Scotland's independence, and, on the other, it is a piece of propaganda. Write a paragraph explaining what the Declaration of Arbroath tells us about Robert Bruce VII's power in Scotland.

4. Create a mind map with at least five people who were involved in the rise and triumph of Robert Bruce VII. Include why each of them was important. Now, change colour and do the same for ten events.

GLOSSARY

Term	Meaning
conscripted	Forcibly called up for the military.
crowning	The act of giving the King the insignia of royalty, on his succeeding to the sovereignty.
excommunication	The action of officially excluding someone from participation in the sacraments and services of the Christian Church.
galley	A low, flat ship with one or more sails and up to three banks of oars, mainly used for warfare.
kindred	One's family and relations.
levy	To enlist (someone) for military service or impose a tax, fee or fine.
litter	A structure used to transport people, containing a bed or seat enclosed by curtains and carried on men's shoulders or by animals.
pater noster	The Lord's Prayer, especially in Latin.
sacrilegious	Involving or committing a crime against a sacred object, place or person.
scutage	In England, money paid by a vassal to his lord instead of military service.

escaped from the city but was captured in Wales on 16 November 1326. He was then imprisoned in Kenilworth Castle. He abdicated in favour of his son, Edward III, on 20 January 1327. He managed to escape, but he was killed, most likely on 21 September 1327, near Gloucestershire to prevent any attempt at his restoration. The assassination of Edward II and the ascendency of Isabella and Mortimer's minority government, for Edward III, removed Bruce's previously powerful opponent and left the new government open to pressure as it established its rule.

Bruce VII now directly intervened in England and put pressure on the new, unstable government by threatening to annex parts of the north of England. This was a direct threat to Edward III's territorial security: the border castles. Bruce took tributes and homages as far south as North Riding in Yorkshire, more than 100 miles south of the Scottish/English border. This put huge pressure on the new regime, and, in October 1327, Isabella and Mortimer opened negotiations with Bruce, fully prepared to offer independence to Scotland and acknowledgement of his right to be King.

On 17 March 1328, the treaty guaranteeing independence was ratified in Edinburgh. On 4 May it was approved by Edward III's parliament at Northampton. Bruce VII was prepared to be generous with the peace; he agreed to pay £20,000 to the new government. Bruce also agreed that David Bruce, his newborn son and heir, should marry Joan, Edward III's sister, to prevent Bruce from looking for a French wife and to secure peace through family ties between the two kingdoms again. Both kingdoms would give each other military aid, except against France, which was still Scotland's political ally. For this, Edward III's government would acknowledge Bruce as King of Scotland and give up all English claims to overlordship of Scotland. It was also agreed that Edward III would put pressure on the Pope to accept Robert Bruce VII as King. In June 1329, the Pope granted the right to be crowned and anointed to Kings of Scots: this gave Scotland the full symbols of independent monarchy for the first time. This was the final element in Bruce's rise and represented his ultimate triumph. It demonstrates that he was internationally recognised as King of Scots and that Scotland was a free country.

It would, however, be wrong to say that attitudes in England had changed in respect of Robert Bruce VII's administration. Many nobles, including Edward III himself, were angry that a peace deal had been made since Bruce was so old and likely to die soon. In his anger, Edward III did not attend his sister's wedding on 17 July 1328. The London mob refused to let the Stone of Destiny be returned to Scotland, as per the terms of the treaty. It would remain in London for another 668 years. Therefore, it is clear that there were many who still believed Scotland should be under the control of the English King.

Robert Bruce, King of Scots for 23 years, died at Cardoss on 7 June 1329. His body, minus its heart and guts, were carried to Dunfermline Abbey and interred next to the other Kings of Scotland. Sir James Douglas went on crusade for Scotland a year later, carrying his King's heart in a silver casket to the Holy Land. Douglas was attacked on his way and, realising he was going to die, threw Bruce's 'braveheart' into the fray. The heart and casket were removed and taken to Melrose Abbey where they were interred.

Bruce's army lost many men in the battle against Hotham. Famine caused starvation among his ranks, forcing them to retreat. However, their presence was still a potential threat to the English-held capital of Ireland, Dublin, not to mention Wales. An English defeat in Ireland would have radically altered the balance of power in Britain. It could have led to England being surrounded by the mutually supportive nations of Wales, Ireland and Scotland.

By March 1316, Scottish forces had advanced to Shannon in south-west Ireland. There was a rumour that Robert Bruce VII was encouraging his brother to make Ireland a satellite state of Scotland by helping Edward Bruce assert himself as King. However, by autumn 1316 Edward II of England had raised an army of 150 mounted cavalry and 500 foot soldiers to expel the Scots from Ireland. The English army landed in Cork in early 1317 and chased the starving Scots back to their base at Ulster. This was a blow to the Scottish regime in Ireland and left Edward Bruce and his men in territory that was significantly more hostile and dangerous than before.

Edward II managed to gather more men in Ireland and clashed with Edward Bruce south of Ulster at the Battle of Faughart in 1318. Here, Edward Bruce was killed and his army defeated. This was a terrible personal and strategic blow to Robert Bruce VII. It marked the end of the Scottish invasion of Ireland as well as their hostilities against the English in Ireland. Despite this, it is fair to argue that the Ireland campaign was overall a success for Bruce in that it continued to embarrass Edward II, proving him unable to expel the invading Scots. It also demonstrated the power of the Bruce regime, which was able to continue occupying land controlled by Edward II for several years. Fighting in Ireland also diverted troops and resources away from England, allowing Bruce more victories in the skirmishes that occurred back and forth across the border between England and Scotland.

After hostilities in Ireland, Robert Bruce VII redoubled his fighting into northern England. However, a famine prevented him from making any serious headway. By 1317, most communities were paying off the Scots to stop them attacking as it was clear Edward II was not coming to their aid. This suggests that continuing his hostilities in the north of England resulted in the submission of the northern community, and money for the Scottish treasury, and demonstrated again that Edward II could not protect the north of England from the Scottish army.

Edward II attempted to raid Berwick in 1319 but was rebuffed by Bruce VII's troops who were sent to York to stop the advance. Further attempts were crushed and James Douglas continued his guerrilla campaign of hit-and-run attacks on English troops in Newcastle. For example, at the Battle of Old Byland on 14 October 1322, Edward II was defeated by Moray and Douglas. The King had to flee to York, abandoning his wife Queen Isabella and his household goods and suffering significant losses in equipment and money. Queen Isabella had to escape by sea from Tynemouth. This campaigning was important because, soon after this, Edward called off his Scottish campaign, and it was clear that some kind of truce was going to have to be made with Bruce as the King of Scots.

4.3 The Declaration of Arbroath, 6 April 1320

In order to be officially recognised as King, Robert Bruce VII had to win the support of the Pope. Pope John XXII did not approve of the Bruce regime. By this point, the Pope had released the Scots from their oaths to Robert Bruce VII and was actively trying to undermine his kingship for a couple of reasons: first, because Bruce had refused to stop fighting with England, despite the fact that the Pope had demanded a ceasefire after 1314; and second, because Bruce had killed John Comyn on sacred

4.2 Continuing hostilities, 1314–28

Robert Bruce VII had won the battle, but he had not won the war. Edward II agreed to call a truce in October 1314, but he still would not acknowledge Bruce's sovereignty as King. Edward II would not capitulate to Bruce's demands after one battle and could easily attack again the next year. Despite John Comyn of Badenoch, the son of the murdered Comyn, and his cousin Walter Comyn having been killed at the Battle of Bannockburn, there was still some opposition to Bruce in Scotland. For example, John of Argyll continued to make trouble for Bruce in the Irish Sea. Bruce would spend 1314 to 1318 securing his victory.

On 6 November 1314, Bruce VII called a parliament at Cambuskenneth Abbey to consolidate his power. He also made his nobles choose to be landholders in either Scotland or England. For example, Neil Campbell of Lochawe was made custodian of all of Atholl's former lands. Bruce also made commitments to solidify Scottish law by conducting investigations into ownership of land and rewriting legal and financial laws. By organising his administration, regranting the lands in Scotland and giving titles to his supporters, Bruce was able to rebuild the Scottish political community. Now he could maintain control in Scotland and continue his hostilities against Edward II.

Bruce VII continued his pressure on Edward II by mounting raids into northern England. England was already suffering under the Great European Famine of 1315–17. Edward was facing political problems. He had fallen out with his nobles after the murder of one of his favourites, Piers Gaveston. Bruce seized this opportunity and sent raiding parties on horseback into Northumbria, Newcastle, Durham and Swaledale. The raiding parties burnt, looted and pillaged on their way, collecting as much plunder as possible. The towns of Brough and Appleby and the castle of Kirkoswald were burnt to the ground. They also stole herds of cattle and trampled across crops at Salkend and then moved to Liddesdale. This was an important element of the continuing hostilities as Bruce secured his regime. Edward did not effectively protect his northern regions. Instead, many resorted to paying off the Scottish raiders to prevent them from routing their land. For example, the people of Copeland in Cumbria paid 600 marks for a guarantee of six months' safety. This made Edward look weak and unable to protect his people. Scottish raids also targeted religious houses where they could take items of more value, such as relics. These raids put more pressure on Edward to negotiate with Bruce.

However, the raids were not enough and, to increase the pressure on Edward II, Edward Bruce was sent to Ireland to attack the English King's forces on two fronts. He landed in Larne in County Antrim on 26 May 1315. Edward Bruce, and several thousand veterans of the Scottish wars, managed to take over key strongholds in just three weeks. Edward Bruce was crowned King of Ireland. This quick march through Ireland made the Bruce regime look strong and like a credible expansionist force, embarrassing Edward II by continuing to occupy Ireland.

Four months after landing, Edward Bruce had taken Ulster, then had further victories in battles at Kells and Skerries in Kildaire. This was a direct threat to the English lordship in Ireland, which English Kings had considered part of their realm since the late twelfth century.

The precarious position of Edward II allowed Edward Bruce three years of military success and allowed the Scottish campaign of expansion the possibility of an attempt to invade Wales. However, by September 1315, John Hotham, an English royal clerk, had arrived in Ireland with men and money to take on the Scottish advance. Edward

On the second day, Sunday 24 June, Edward II's army was exhausted. They had been forced to move and protect their camp in the night in fear of a Scottish attack, so had not recovered from their march north. Bruce VII gave a speech to his men to motivate them and awarded knighthoods to Walter Stewart and James Douglas. The Scots knelt and said a **pater noster**, the Lord's Prayer, and were blessed by Abbot Maurice of Inchaffray before the battle began. This kept morale high. Determination to fight was key to their victory as the troops would be encouraged to follow orders and not break ranks.

Figure 4.8 Maurice, the Abbot of Inchaffray, blessing Bruce's troops before the Battle of Bannockburn in 1314. This image was created in 1890, although its creator is unknown. It is clear that this illustrator had Scottish sympathies as they portrayed the Scots as devout Christians, receiving blessings before going into battle.

The conflict started with archers exchanging volleys of arrows, but the narrowness of the field made it hard for the English army to organise their ranks effectively. Then the Scottish army advanced with two schiltrons next to each other, with Bruce VII's schiltron behind them. This helped Bruce win as the advance of the Scottish infantry was quick and Edward II's forces were taken by surprise, causing confusion within the ranks of the English army.

The Earl of Gloucester led Edward II's infantry forward to meet Edward Bruce's schiltron. The schiltron attack was effective. Horses and riders were either impaled or thrown from their mounts. Gloucester's horse was killed underneath him and he fell to his death. This was a decisive moment in the battle as the charge broke down without their leading noble. Other nobles, including Sir Robert Clifford, were knocked or dragged from their horses. Without effective noble leadership in its ranks, Edward II's army became confused and less effective as a fighting force against Bruce's.

Edward II's archers were crammed in behind their cavalry and so continued to be ineffective. At this point, according to some accounts, yeomen, caterers and labourers from the Scottish army who had been guarding Bruce's baggage train came over the hill, thinking that, given all the noise, the battle had been won and was over. These people have become known as the 'Sma' Folk' (or 'Small Folk'). They were of such low standing that they were not expected to serve in the army, but now they were mistaken for a further Scottish army. Unable to mount an effective charge, and faced with what they thought was another wave of Bruce's force charging down the hill, Edward's army fell back against the Bannock Burn, falling over one another in an effort to retreat. Some parts of the drop to the burn were 4 metres deep and many of Edward's men drowned as they tried to retreat.

> ### SOURCE 2
>
> When both armies engaged each other and the great horses of the English charged the pikes of the Scots like into a dense forest, there arose a great and terrible crash of spears broken and of the horses wounded to death. Now the English in the rear could not reach the Scots because the leading division was in the way, nor could they do anything to help themselves, so there was nothing for it but to take flight.
>
> In the leading division the Earl of Gloucester, Sir John Comyn, Sir Pain Tiptoft, Sir Edmund Mauley and many other nobles were killed, besides foot soldiers who fell in great numbers. Another calamity which befell the English was that whereas they had shortly before crossed a great ditch called Bannockburn, into which the tide flows, they now wanted to recross it; in confusion, many nobles and others fell into it with their horse in the crush, while others escaped with much difficulty, and many were never able to extricate themselves from the ditch.
>
> **A description of the Battle of Bannockburn (day 2), from the *Lanercost Chronicle*.**

This secured victory in battle for Bruce VII, and Edward II was led from the field by the Earl of Pembroke. The victory should not have been possible against such a large army and was an important turning point in the rise and triumph of Robert Bruce VII. He had beaten Edward II, the English King, in pitched battle and removed the English soldiers and nobles from Scotland. News of his victory travelled fast around Europe.

The garrison commander at Stirling Castle, Mowbray, would not let Edward II into the castle. This was a shrewd move which probably prevented the English King from being captured. Instead, Edward retreated to Dunbar Castle, chased by James Douglas all the way, where he escaped to Berwick by ship. This was a blow for Bruce. Ideally, if Edward had not been killed in battle, he would have been captured and taken prisoner to force him into accepting Robert Bruce VII as King of Scots.

However, Bruce VII did manage to take over 75 political prisoners to ransom, including the Earl of Angus, Sir Ingram de Umfraville. Bruce was able to ransom these prisoners according to their rank and use them to negotiate the release of other prisoners who were on his side. For example, the Earl of Hereford was exchanged for the return of Bishop Wishart of Glasgow, Bishop Lamberton of St Andrews and the Bruce women who had been captured some seven years before. This was important for Bruce as he was able to secure the return of important clerical, military, political and familial members of his party. These were people who would be key to providing council and in securing the future of the Bruce bloodline. Both of these factors were hugely important in ensuring his reign would be secure.

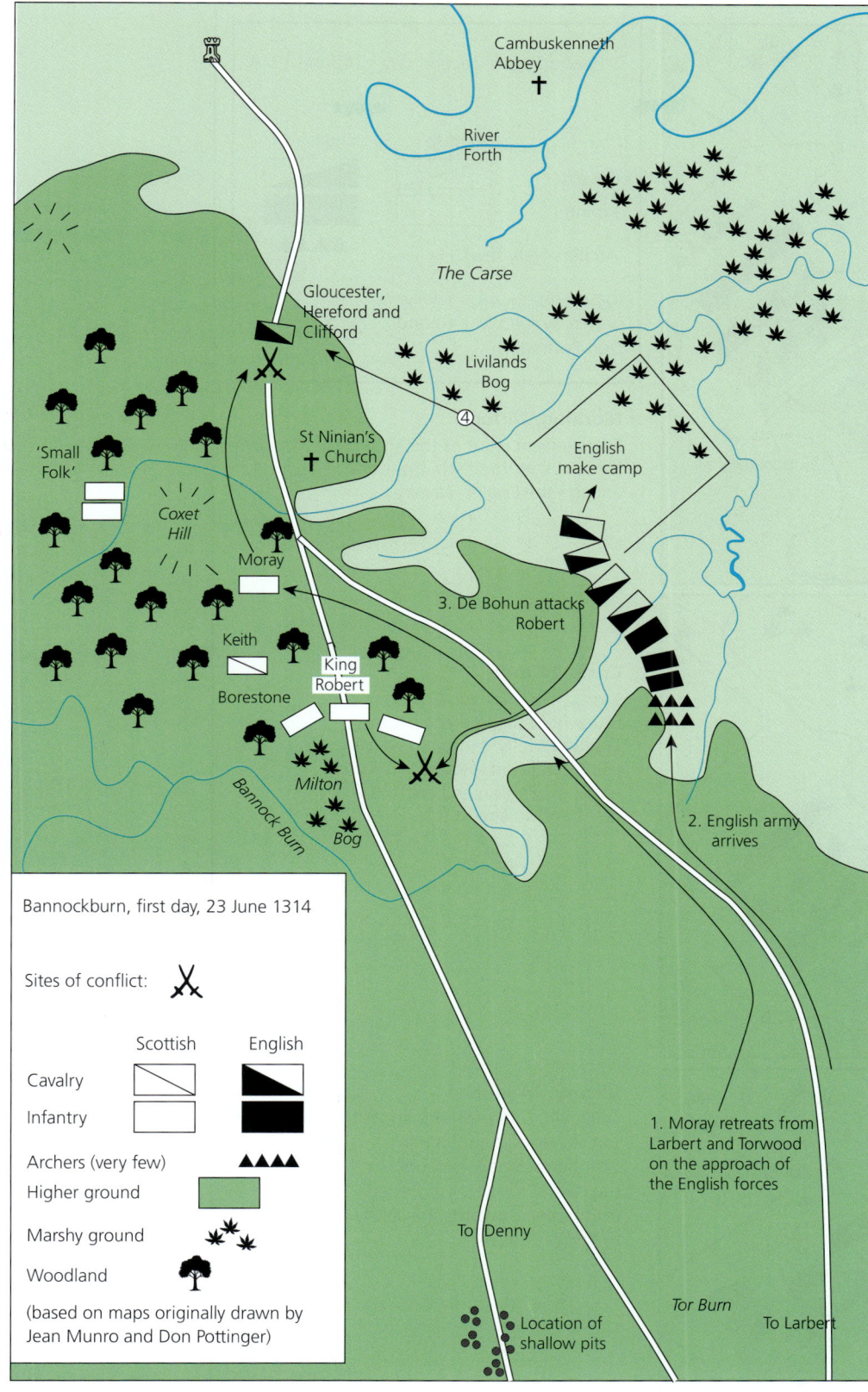

Figure 4.7 Army placement and movement at the Battle of Bannockburn.

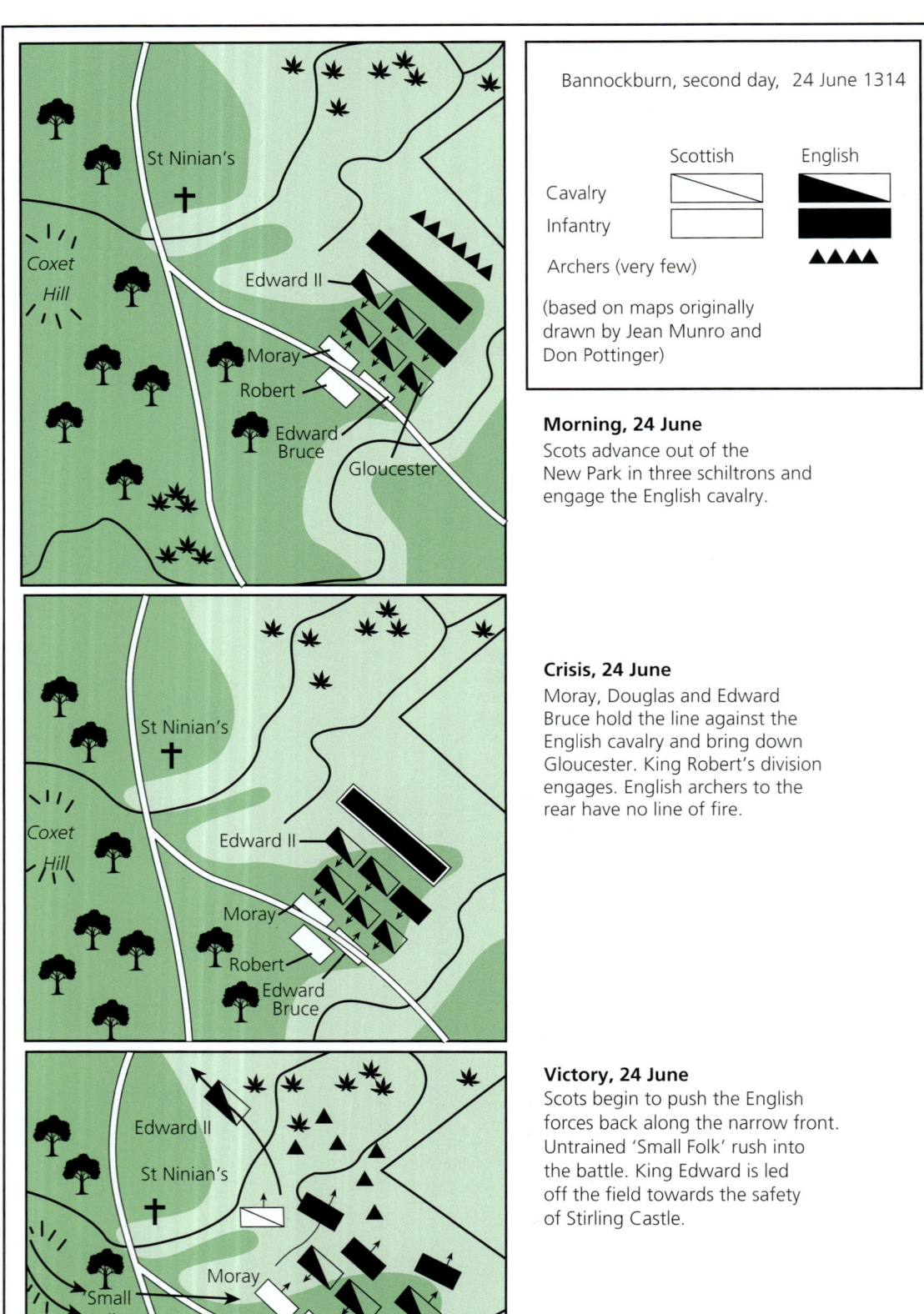

Figure 4.7 (cont.) Army placement and movement at the Battle of Bannockburn.

> **SOURCE 3**
>
> But from these innumerable evils [of Edward I] we have been freed with the help of our most valiant prince, king and lord the lord Robert, who in order that his people and his inheritance might be delivered out of the hands of enemies, cheerfully endured toil and fatigue, hunger and danger ...
>
> We are bound to him for the maintenance of our freedom both by his right and his merits, as to the one by whom deliverance has been wrought unto our people, and come what may we mean to stand by him. Yet if he should give up what he has begun, seeking to make us or our kingdom subject to the king of England or to the English we would exert ourselves at once to drive him out as our enemy and as a subverter of his own right and ours and we would make some other man who was able to defend us as our king. For as long as a hundred of us remain alive, we will never on any conditions be subjected to the lordship of the English. For we fight not for glory or riches or honours, but for freedom alone, which no good man gives up except with his life.
>
> **An extract from the Declaration of Arbroath, which claimed to be from the barons, free landholders and the 'whole community of the realm' of Scotland to the Pope. It was written in Latin at the Abbey of Arbroath on 6 April 1320. The title 'Declaration of Arbroath' has only been used in modern times.**

There were still, however, some nobles who opposed Bruce VII. Patrick, Earl of Dunbar, who was in France, heard about a plot to assassinate Bruce, known as the Soules conspiracy. This was a plan to overthrow Bruce and reinstall the Balliol family. With his brother, Edward Bruce, dead and his daughter, Marjorie Bruce, dead through childbirth, Bruce's heir was his four-year-old grandson, Robert Stewart. The King was 46, and there were still Scots who believed that the crown should be with the Balliol family, so his reign still faced opposition, even if much of that was secret.

Bruce VII dealt quickly with those who had conspired to remove him from the throne in the Soules conspiracy. For example, the conspirators were tried by parliament in 1318. This was the first time the Scottish parliament had been used for a treason trial and the first time anyone had been tried for treason against a King of Scots. Bruce and his government had been developing a more heightened idea of what it was to be a King. While some were acquitted, Sir David Brechin was executed. He had not been an active conspirator but had known about the plan and not told the King. Bruce's merciless and swift actions were key to ensuring that the triumph of his rise to the throne would be maintained by his dynasty after his death.

4.4 The Treaties of Edinburgh/Northampton, 1328

In 1328, Robert Bruce VII was finally able to get the King of England to acknowledge Scotland as independent and Bruce as its rightful King. Bruce was now old and dying, perhaps of leprosy, but would see Scotland become an independent country before his death. The Pope had stated that he could not recognise Bruce's kingship until Edward II's regime had recognised him as King. So, this acknowledgement from the King of England was an important element of Bruce's triumph and rise to power.

By 1328, Edward II had been overthrown by his Queen, Queen Isabella, and her partner, Lord Mortimer. This cleared the way for Bruce VII to be acknowledged as King of Scots. Isabella landed from France with a small force in England in September 1326 and, within a month, had taken London from Edward II. Edward II ground. Gaining papal approval was important because it would put an end to the possibility of John Balliol's son, Edward Balliol, returning to power. Edward Balliol was in the English court and had not been allowed to go with his father into exile. After Bruce's, and the clergy of his government's, attempts to change his mind, the Pope finally wrote to Edward II in July 1320 and encouraged him to make peace with Bruce.

The Declaration of Arbroath was a document with the seals of 51 nobles which was sent to the Pope. The Declaration was a carefully crafted piece of political propaganda that gave expression to the rights of the Scottish nation. It falsified the recent parts of Scottish history to state that King Robert I was the undisputed and chosen ruler of Scotland. It also claimed that if Bruce stopped acting in the interests of the realm, then the Scots would come together to drive him out as an enemy. This was, of course, cleverly fashioned by Bruce to excuse his past murder and validate his blood claim, despite the decision taken at Norham in 1292.

It is, however, also reasonable to assume the Declaration expressed how some members of the Scottish community felt about the Bruce kingship. Scotland had been without an internationally and domestically accepted King for almost 30 years. In this time, the nobility had become used to ruling in the absence of a King and were in a far more powerful position than before. It seems reasonable that they would have wanted some control over who would rule them. However, there is no doubt that the Declaration was not a unanimously agreed document and that it was used to lobby the Pope to gain papal legitimacy for Bruce's regime. Although this failed, the document became an important statement of the success, power and rightfulness of Bruce as King and of Scotland as an independent nation.

Figure 4.9 The Declaration of Arbroath, with the seals of the Scottish nobility attached.